THE SHARK IS ROARING

The Shark is Roaring – The Story of Jaws: The Revenge

BearManor Media
2022

The Shark is Roaring – The Story of Jaws: The Revenge

First Printing Edition, 2022

All rights reserved.

No portion of this publication may be reproduced, stored, and/or copied electronically (except for academic use as a source), nor transmitted in any form or by any means without the prior written permission of the publisher and/or author.

This book is an independent editorial work and is not authorised by or affiliated with NBCUniversal or any other entity related to the Jaws series. The photos contained within are copyright of their respective owners and appear here only to illustrate the points of the commentary and criticism within the text.

Published in the United States of America by:

BearManor Media

4700 Millenia Blvd.
Suite 175 PMB 90497
Orlando, FL 32839

bearmanormedia.com

Printed in the United States.

Typesetting and layout by BearManor Media

Cover Art by Brendan Haley @haleydoodles

Available from https://usedtotech.com and other retail outlets

ISBN—978-1-62933-972-6

Contents

1. Introduction — 1
2. The Genesis of Jaws: The Revenge — 5
3. The Original Jaws IV — 8
4. Jaws '87 is Announced — 10
5. Casting Jaws '87 — 16
6. Roy Scheider Turns Down Return — 27
7. Return to Amity — 28
8. Bahamas Bound — 33
9. Filming at Universal — 47
10. From Script to Screen — 53
11. The Characters — 60
12. Michael Caine and the Oscar Debacle — 70
13. Spielberg Gives His Blessing — 72
14. The Press Circuit Starts — 73
15. Reviews and Critical Response — 77
16. Release — 81
17. Taking a Bite out of the Razzies — 86
18. Jaws: The Revenge Exhumed — 88
19. Alternative Cuts — 103
20. Scoring Jaws: The Revenge — 109
21. Joseph Sargent reflects on Revenge — 118
22. The Novelisation — 121

23. Digesting Jaws: The Revenge	124
24. The Tragedy of Judith Barsi	133
25. Jaws the NES Game	140
26. Jaws The Worst by B. Harrison Smith	145
27. Shark Movies Post-Revenge	152
28. Interviews	158
29. The Legacy of Jaws: The Revenge	184
Index	189

"I haven't seen it, but I've seen the house
that it bought my mother and it's marvelous."
Michael Caine on Jaws: The Revenge

Introduction

Bruce Junior takes the bait

Notoriously Jaws: The Revenge is the only film on Rotten Tomatoes with a 0% score, but does it warrant such loathing?

Released in 1987, the film came at an interesting time in the Hollywood studio system with sequels now commonplace, ironically with this wave kicked off by Jaws 2 in 1978.

The ingredients were in place for another summer blockbuster for Universal. With an Oscar-nominated star in Michael Caine plus the returning Lorraine Gary from the first two films and a return to Edgartown (Amity itself), the aim was for a more back-to-basics Jaws, following the dip in box office takings for Jaws 3D (making $88 million compared to Jaws 2's $208 million) in 1983.

Universal Studios President Sid Sheinberg gave the production what seemed like an open cheque for production on the proviso that a summer 1987 release date could be achieved. So what went wrong? This is what I will explore here.

From being a huge fan of Spielberg's classic as a young child, I also became strangely enamored with its sequels; but most notoriously Jaws: The Revenge.

When you are young, even as a horror fan there are some scenes you can't stomach and two distinctly stand out for me. Quint's death in Jaws plus Sean Brody's demise in the opening of Revenge. I can distinctly recall having to cover my eyes with a cushion during both scenes but it has to be said Mitchell Anderson's guttural screams as the shark rips his arm off before killing him lived long in my dreams for years to come.

As my tenth birthday approached I asked my mum for the VHS tapes of Jaws and Jaws: The Revenge and I can recall playing them on loop during that warm summer day in July of 1994 when I probably should have been playing in the sunshine.

In the intervening years, Revenge would play regularly on BBC One with the promotional trailer always making the film look far better than it actually was. Safe to say I tuned in most of the time and the film became a guilty pleasure that I became less and less ashamed about as the years passed.

Now 35 years later I have attempted to put together a comprehensive account of how Jaws: The Revenge came into existence and discuss what its legacy is.

This book features analysis of the filming, the characters, the soundtrack, the infamous novelisation, the shooting script, alternate cuts of the film plus interviews with cast and crew who share details of what it was like to film. I also attempt to pay tribute to the late Judith Barsi, with a chapter focused on her extremely sad and premature demise shortly after Revenge was released, in what was probably the toughest and emotional chapter to write.

We also have a bonus chapter from filmmaker and podcaster B. Harrison Smith, who takes a more cynical look at the creation of the film and how financial gain may have overtaken creative instincts at Universal.

I hope you enjoy reading this as much as I enjoyed writing it.

Paul Downey – Author.

The Genesis of Jaws: The Revenge

The acting career of Lorraine Gary appeared to be over after her small role in 1941, directed by Steven Spielberg. Following this film, the actress admitted that the phone did stop ringing, which led to her taking a role as a Literary Agent, which she undertook until 1984.

After quitting this role she began doing volunteer work with mentally ill children and started to lead a more leisurely existence. Little did she know that another encounter with a vengeful shark was just around the corner...

In September 1986 director Joseph Sargent was approached by Gary's husband, MCA President Sidney Sheinberg, about directing the fourth installment in the Jaws franchise.

The killer shark series had been dormant for three years at this point, after the critically panned Jaws 3D in 1983. Sheinberg without a script at this point was looking for a director who could turn around the project within nine months, with an ambitious target of summer 1987 for a theatrical release.

Sheinberg appeared to take inspiration from James Cameron's Aliens, which saw the return of Sigourney Weaver as Ellen Ripley, a strong female lead battling a seemingly unstoppable creature, or in this case creatures. Sound familiar?

With audiences clambering for more xenomorph action (Aliens grossed $130 million worldwide), Sheinberg believed that by thrusting his wife front and centre the Jaws franchise could be resurrected from its watery grave.

Sargent discussed the genesis of the project with the LA Times in a press feature in February 1987,

"I didn't have time to laugh, because Sid explained he wanted to do a quality picture about human beings. When he told me, 'It's your baby, you produce and direct,' I accepted."

Sargent would now hire writer Michael De Guzman to put the script together whilst he assembled a cast. De Guzman was known to Universal at the time, having penned two episodes of the Spielberg-produced Amazing Stories that same year.

De Guzman met with Sheinberg and was then shocked to discover a two page spread in Variety formally announcing the tentatively titled Jaws '87.

"We were left hanging. Next thing I knew, I picked up Variety and was stunned – a two-page colour spread announced 'Jaws 1987' and that I was writing and Sargent was producing and directing."

De Guzman also noted that Universal was planning on spending millions ($23 million in total) for building the shark models, handing out contracts and hiring special effects people despite the fact at this stage the script had not even started. The writer would turn around the script within five weeks of being hired, although the final shooting script was completed during production.

Sheinberg, himself was looking to bring Jaws back to its roots, discarding the narratives established in Jaws 2 and Jaws 3D (which he called 'a pretty bad movie'), saying,

"The people running Universal motion pictures at that time (the Price regime) couldn't get the 'Jaws' notion off the ground.

"The only way to get another 'Jaws' done was to take direct responsibility myself. I got the kind of people I knew (who) could work fast and well with the 'Jaws' premise. It was done in a very unconventional manner."

Sheinberg was hopeful that a back-to-basics approach would lead to box office dollars.

"This is a more human story, he said, than any of the previous 'Jaws' films. The script and the picture should make you laugh and cry and give you a few good scares in between because of its quality.

We have very high expectations for its commercial success," he told Calendar.

The wheels were now rolling for Jaws '87.

The Original Jaws IV

Screenwriter Steve De Jarnatt was first approached about writing the script for Jaws IV, with a very different concept than what we saw from Michael De Guzman and Joseph Sargent.

The budding writer was on Universal's radar after penning 4 episodes of the '80s reboot of the Alfred Hitchcock Presents series.

Universal offered De Jarnatt the chance to re-invigorate the series following the disappointment of Jaws 3D. He was given an office on the backlot near Amblin, but during this time (circa 1985 according to De Jarnatt) he went to direct sci-fi action feature Cherry 2000.

De Jarnatt was hired by the new Universal Head of Production Frank Price, who had overseen the TV branch of the studio across the 1970s, with hit shows such as The Six Million Dollar Man, The Incredible Hulk, Battlestar Galactica and The Rockford Files.

He left for Columbia Pictures in 1978 and had great success with blockbusters such as Gandhi, Ghostbusters and The Karate Kid. His brief tenure at Universal began in 1983 and it was his open attitude to the next Jaws sequel which excited De Jarnatt.

"He was open to anything and not necessarily following a template. My idea was to set the film in Malibu with surf punks (kind of a Hollywood Inside story) and the studio was interested," De Jarnatt said.

The film never got beyond the development stage as Frank Price and Universal CEO Sid Sheinberg allegedly ended up in a fist fight which resulted in Price being fired and De Jarnatt's script being canned.

But what did the script look like? De Jarnatt provides this insight into his Jaws 4,

"It was way better than the Jaws 4 that got made and was probably on par with Sharknado (I joke). I haven't read it in 35 years but I can recall the opening scene as it mirrored the original, to some degree.

"This is a period piece in merry old England, as a wench and a squire are drunk on the beach with flutes playing in the distance. She peels off her corset and swims out as he remains onshore.

"She begins to flail and yell and we hear the signature Jaws theme and we cut to a POV of a huge shark rising up towards her. We then cut to another view below the shark rising and at the last second, a shark five times bigger (predating Megalodon) bites the first shark in half. The girl screams as blood and guts float up around her and we reveal that this is set in the present-day at The Renaissance Fair in Malibu.

"I remember the lead character got swallowed whole and needed to cut his way out of the shark.

"Frank Price only handed me one note saying there needed to be a scene where the shark comes up through a disco dance floor at an expensive house built over the waves.

"They liked it but it ended in a millisecond when Frank Price and Sid (Sheinberg) got in a fistfight. My version was then officially dead."

The official statement from Universal on 17th September 1986 said that Frank Price has resigned, following disappointing box office receipts for Legal Eagles and Howard the Duck.

An anonymous producer at Universal told Variety,

"A duck brought Price down. An innocent, lovable duck."

But does De Jarnatt think any idea could have saved the Jaws franchise at this stage?

"Who the hell knows," he quipped.

Jaws '87 Is Announced

Cameras get ready to roll on Jaws '87

The Associated Press received a press release on 6th November 1986 which announced that Jaws '87 would be hitting cinemas next summer. The only details known at this stage were that MCA President Sidney Sheinberg would produce the film, with his wife and Jaws alumni Lorraine Gary returning to acting for the first time since Steven Spielberg's 1941.

In December it was revealed by Massachusetts Film Bureau spokeswoman Terri Morris that Universal Pictures would be returning to Martha's Vineyard to film the then-titled Jaws '87 early next year.

The first portion of the production was revealed to be taking place in Edgartown before heading to the Bahamas for a larger portion of the scenes.

"They are scouting the locations right now," Morris said.

"I know they will be using the centre of the town, beach areas and private homes."

Executive Producer Frank Baur was also quoted saying,

"We are delighted to be returning to Martha's Vineyard. It gives us continuity from Jaws to Jaws '87."

Morris also informed the press that Lorraine Gary would be returning to the role of Ellen Brody and that Universal Pictures was still negotiating to get Roy Scheider to also return as her on-screen husband and twice-saviour of Amity – Martin Brody.

Gary admitted to being in a state of 'depression and panic' during the first days of rehearsal, although she settled and started to enjoy being in the spotlight once again.

"This role is what I used to dream of, until I became happy as a person, no longer depending on acting to be fulfilled," Gary told Donna Rosenthal of the LA Times.

On 26th December 1986 Montana-based newspaper The Missoulian reported that Industrial Light & Magic would be tasked with bringing the animatronic great white shark to life for the film having recently wrapped on the fourth entry of the Star Trek series – The Voyage Home.

"Industrial Light & Magic, creators of the whale (from Star Trek IV) are working on the makeover reports," confirmed producer/director Joseph Sargent.

The Tampa Tribune also reported ILM's involvement in Jaws 4 on 1st January 1987, noting that the shark would be 25 feet in length (the same length noted by Quint in the original film).

"The ILM shark will just be used for the sequences where we need a self-propelled creation, like some underwater shots," Joseph Sargent commented.

Interestingly, the same news report also noted that the budget was around $15 million, whereas the finished picture ended up costing $23 million.

Writer Michael De Guzman spoke to Cinefantastique's Bill Kelley for their January issue, confirming that Jaws 3D's storyline would be discarded in favour of a narrative more closely aligned to the Spielberg film.

"It will be a serious movie by returning to some of the Benchley book and the Spielberg movie.

"Jaws 3D is not even recognised by Sheinberg. He's embarrassed by it. In this film we are taking into account the growth factor – the original audience has grown up," De Guzman said.

The other interesting anecdote in this article, states that shooting would take place in Australia or the Caribbean, according to Sargent, to save money on the initially reported $15 million budget.

Production was clearly moving at a pace behind the scenes, with a press release widely circulated to newspapers from 3rd January 1987, saying that studio executives from Universal were now scouting backgrounds in Edgartown ahead of the start of filming for Jaws '87. According to Donna Rosenthal in the LA Times, Universal would pay $10,000 to cover permits, site rentals and administration.

Word of the Jaws production started to spread in Edgartown, with Cape Cod Times writer Ricky Fleury reporting that over 300 people had turned up to the Kelley House on Monday 5th January to try and get the chance to be in Jaws '87.

There were rumours amongst attendees that the production crew were also looking for someone to play Sean Brody (the role played by Mitchell Anderson), but this was quickly debunked when it was revealed that the role had already been cast.

Fleury also revealed that On Location...the Making of Jaws author Edith Blake was serving as an assistant casting director for the Edgartown segment of filming. Her role consisted of taking photographs of each of the 300 attendees and passing them onto the casting team to decide who would make the cut.

Two days later Fleury talked to a number of Edgartown residents who were auditioning as extras for Jaws '87.

Fleury does describe the film as starring Roy Scheider, who had been negotiating with Universal Pictures but ultimately would turn them down.

Martha Campbell who auditioned for the role of Tiffany, the wife-to-be of Sean Brody said,

"It was a little scary, but it was fun. It depends (on) how important this is to you."

Another aspiring actress Rhonda Steere of Vineyard Haven was willing to go the extra mile in dying her hair to bag the part of Tiffany.

"I think I have a good chance. Janice Hull told me to wait a minute, sit back down. This would be a nice birthday present (as it's my birthday in two days)," she said.

Both Martha and Rhonda would be left disappointed with the role of Tiffany being secured by actress Mary Smith.

Pre-production for the scenes in the Bahamas would begin on 12th January 1987 with Special Effects Supervisor Henry Millar and his team arriving at South Beach in Nassau where testing would begin on the animatronic shark models.

"Two models were fully articulated, two were made for jumping, one for ramming, one was a half-shark (the top half) and one was just a fin," Millar commented in the production notes.

"The two fully articulated models each had 22 sectioned ribs and movable jaws covered by a flexible water-based latex skin, measured 25 feet (7.6 m) in length and weighed 2500 pounds. Each tooth was half a foot long and as sharp as it looked. All models were housed undercover...in a secret location on the island."

Edith Blake, writing for the Vineyard Gazette on 23rd January updated readers on the progress of pre-production for the fourth Jaws film saying that production had been established at the Wharf Restaurant in Edgartown plus The Kelley House, Heritage Hotel and Governor Bradford Inn which had been completed sold out by the Universal team.

J. William Hudgins from the Edgartown Marine was recruited to find boats, with specific instructions to find a smaller boat that would be used in Sean Brody's attack scene at the opening of the film.

The Vineyard Gazette would double as the Amity Police station with Memorial Wharf being used for a larger scale Christmas scene, with carolers singing Christmas songs.

Blake also noted that Casting Director Janice Hull was concerned about long hours of shooting given the ice-cold temperatures during February in Edgartown, with potentially 10 hours of shooting for extras, between 1 pm and 11 pm.

Regarding the special effects needed to bring Revenge's shark to life, animator Ted Rae and his company Little Buddy Productions approached Sargent about working on the filming, having provided stop-motion for Jaws 3D in 1983.

Talking to the 28th October 1987 edition of The Hollywood Reporter, Rae said,

"I just called up director Joseph Sargent's office and said, 'Look I don't know how you go about this, but I worked on the last movie; we did some good stuff, and I think we can help you. They said, 'Fine, come on in.'"

At this pre-production stage, serious consideration was given for ILM to create a miniature free-swimming shark that would echo the Orca seen in Star Trek IV.

"We were talking about having a shark in the same scene as a character. Other than a few isolated shots in Orca (the 1977 Jaws-ploitation feature directed by Michael Anderson), I've never seen anything like that – I mean nobody's crazy enough to get in the water with a real Great White!" he told the September 1987 edition of Cinefantastique.

Rae would be assisted by Little Buddy technicians Tim Lawrence and Peter Folkens, who would combine their expertise in plastics and mould systems and ichthyology respectively to create composite drawings based on the measurements of three great white sharks.

Rae's work would have needed to match the mechanical shark being designed by Henry Millar plus potential real shark footage that was being considered for use during pre-production. Despite his work being approved, it was vetoed after it didn't match up with the mechanical shark's appearance.

"That's because the production's mechanical shark looks like a concrete log with teeth," he quipped to Cinefantastique.

"It's lumpy and doesn't look as good as the shark in the first film."

Around this time Sargent also decided to turn away from using real shark footage, as the difference between the models being built and actually great whites was extremely noticeable.

One of the original scenes pitched for using the miniatures was the shark attacking Michael in the underwater submarine. Arguably, one of the best sequences in the finished film.

The wheels were officially in motion on multiple locations for Jaws '87, but who would be the new characters set to become shark bait this time around?

Casting Jaws '87

Lorraine Gary, Mario Van Peebles and Judith Barsi behind the scenes

With Roy Scheider firmly out of the picture for Jaws '87, the only main cast member from previous films would be Lorraine Gary, taking on a more prominent role as Ellen Brody.

The job of casting the film would go to Casting Director Nancy Nayor, who at this point in her career had only worked on Psycho III, the year previous and Howard The Duck, the film which allegedly killed Frank Price's career at Universal. Now a staple of the industry, she would go on to work on nearly 200 films to date, including Casper, reboots for My Bloody Valentine and Last House on the Left plus Scream 4.

In the joint-lead role Lance Guest was cast as Michael Brody, having accumulated a healthy roster of television work including stints on Lou Grant, St. Elsewhere and ABC Afterschool Specials. He would also be recognisable to genre fans from his role in Halloween II (1981) as ambulance driver Jimmy and his leading role in 1984's The Last Starfighter, which was directed by the original Michael Myers actor from Halloween, Nick Castle.

Talking to the Be More Super Podcast in May 2021, Guest revealed he didn't audition for the role of Michael Brody and was instead just offered the role.

"It was originally called Jaws 87, I didn't audition for it. They just straight up offered me the part and I had been doing plays earlier that year (1986), and I hadn't done a movie in a long time. I read the script and I was like, this is great, what a great part. They really fleshed the guy out and he really carries the movie."

New Jersey-born actress Karen Young would take on the role of Guest's on-screen wife Carla, having previously starred in 9 and Half Weeks and the Burt Reynolds vehicle Heat, not to be confused with the Michael Mann crime drama starring Robert De Niro and Al Pacino.

The career of Mario Van Peebles was starting to take off when he was cast as Jake for Jaws '87. The Mexican-born actor was a mainstay in the NBC series LA Law as Andrew Taylor, with his involvement in the Jaws series seen as a notable benchmark at the time. Van Peebles would go on to have a prolific career on the big and small screen with notable roles in New Jack City (1991), Ali (2001) and more recently in TV series' Nashville, Z Nation and Empire.

One of the caveats for Van Peebles coming on-board with Jaws 4 was his request to cast his father, who played the minor role of Mr Witherspoon, the Mayor of Nassau.

Michael Caine's career was in a strange place when the opportunity to be part of the fourth Jaws film presented itself. As we know now, he would win an Oscar for Best Supporting Actor for 1986's Hannah and Her Sisters plus starring in Mona Lisa with Bob Hoskins plus Sweet Liberty with one Michelle Pfeiffer.

He would take on the role of Hoagie Newcombe, citing that the script was more human-focused than previous Jaws sequels plus it would be a film his daughter would finally go and see.

Child actress Judith Barsi was a veteran of nearly 20 productions by the time she was cast in what would become Jaws: The Revenge as Thea Brody. She had done a slew of commercials, plus television work on Remington Steele, The Twilight Zone and Cagney and Lacey plus a role on St. Elsewhere, which as previously mentioned featured her Jaws on-screen father Lance Guest between 1982 and 1983 as Sean Rooney. Barsi would go on to provide voicework on classic animated films The Land Before Time and All Dogs Go To Heaven before her life was tragically cut short at the age of 10 when she was shot in a murder-suicide alongside her mother Maria by her father Jozsef Barsi on 25th July 1988.

Mitchell Anderson was another actor who had built up a steady stream of television roles before being cast in Jaws '87. This included spots on Cagney and Lacey in 1985, a year before Judith Barsi who played Shauna Bard in the 1986 episode Disenfranchised. Post-Revenge Anderson would continue to work in television most notably as Dr Jack McGuire in Doogie Howser, M.D, appearing in 51 episodes and a notable role in teen drama Party Of Five, which also featured Matthew Fox (Lost), Neve Campbell (Scream 1-5), Scott Wolf and Jennifer Love Hewitt (The Ghost Whisperer and I Know What You Did Last Summer). After a career break of 16 years, he returned to acting in 2018, starring in the web series After Forever for Days of Our Lives and Friday the 13th alumni Kevin Spirtas.

The Cagney and Lacey connection continued with the casting of Lynn Whitfield as Jake's wife Louisa. Whitfield had also had roles in Hill Street Blues, Miami Vice and The Fall Guy, starring Lee Majors.

For the minor role of Sean Brody's wife-to-be Tiffany, Mary Smith was cast having only one credit to her name; the 1982 western feature Plainsong which was the sole directing credit of editor Ed Stabile, who had previously worked on Big Trouble in Little China and Jumpin' Jack Flash and would go on to work on Steven Seagal's Under Siege and 2001's Moulin Rouge.

In the local newspapers of Edgartown, it is noted that some budding actresses were supposedly auditioning for the role of Tiffany, but it is unclear if Smith was part of this casting process or was brought in by Nayor, or someone on the production specifically for the part.

Clarence, one of the assistant's aboard Neptune's Folly was played by Cedric Scott who had also racked up roles in Starsky and Hutch and Fantasy Island and worked as recently as 2015 with a concierge role in Bound starring Buffy the Vampire Slayer's Charisma Carpenter.

Their second assistant William was played by Charles Bowleg, a Nassau local, in his only acting role. Bowleg ran the DVD store The Movie Zone in Nassau between 2004 and 2020 before it closed permanently.

The final notable cast member is stuntwoman Diane Hetfield, who played the role of Mrs Ferguson, the ill-fated victim of the shark in the banana boat attack sequence. Hetfield's career began in 1984 with a small swimming role, ironically in the crime drama series Matt Houston, starring Lee Horsley (The Hateful Eight). Her stunt work began a year later in Girls Just Wanna Have Fun (starring Sex and the City's Sarah Jessica Parker) plus Friday the 13th Part VI: Jason Lives and Lethal Weapon before she was cast in Jaws: The Revenge. Her stunt career ended in 1991 having also worked most notably on Sean S. Cunningham's DeepStar Six plus James Cameron's The Abyss.

Lee Fierro would reprise her role as Mrs Kintner for Jaws: The Revenge, having worked as a drama teacher in Edgartown in the years between the original and this fourth entry in the series. Fierro would also be part of tours of the Jaws filming locations in the intervening years with fellow Revenge extra Donna Honig. Fierro passed away in 2020 at the age of 91 due to complications with COVID-19.

The role of Polly, the administrator of Amity Police Department was recast for Jaws '87 with local Edna Billotto replacing Peggy Scott who played the role in Spielberg's film.

The final Edgartown Jaws alumni to return to the series was Fritzi Jane Courtney who played Mrs Taft in the original, most notably asking Chief Brody if he is going to close the beaches following the death of Alex Kitner. She would return in Jaws 2 before appearing at the Brody house to greet Michael and his family following Sean's death at the start of the film.

In another connection to the Halloween and Friday the 13th series', stuntman Tom Morga did some stunt work on Jaws 4, although it is unclear what role he doubled for. Morga played the role of the imposter Jason Voorhees in Friday the 13th Part V: A New Beginning plus briefly played Michael Myers in Halloween 4: The Return of Michael Myers before being replaced by George P. Wilbur. Morga would continue stunt work until 2011, with notable roles in the Pirates of the Caribbean series plus a slew of work on Star Trek: The Next Generation.

Another notable part of the stunt cast was legendary stunt coordinator Roydon Clark, who is believed to have doubled for Michael Caine during the finale of the film. Clark was known for his work on Con Air, The Rock, Escape from New York, Ghostbusters II plus a slew of westerns in the 1960s.

Contrary to rumours on IMDB, Jeffrey Kramer, who had played Deputy Hendricks in the first and second Jaws films, was never approached by casting to reprise his role in Jaws: The Revenge. Kramer did, however, work alongside Michael Brody actor Lance Guest in Halloween II (1981) but the pair would not share a scene together.

The main cast take break whilst filming the finale of the film

The Production Crew

When assembling the production crew for Jaws: The Revenge, Universal would go for a mix of experience and youth; with the thinking that the older heads had the tricks of the trade to call upon whereas the younger members of the crew could work at a pace to ensure the July 1987 release was met.

Joining Joseph Sargent as an Associate Producer would be Frank Baur who had worked in numerous roles across film and television. His career began in 1949 as an Associate Producer of the comedy feature Almost a Bride, which starred Shirley Temple. He would also try his hand at directing, with his last project working behind the camera being four episodes of the WWII series The Rat Patrol between 1967 and 1968.

Baur was quoted during the production of Jaws IV, saying that this would be the fastest film he would ever work on. Ironically, this would mark the final work of his career in Hollywood, before he died in 1993 aged 75.

Cinematographer John McPherson was another steady pair of hands well known to the Universal stalwarts, having worked on Spielberg's Amazing Stories series for 13 episodes between 1985 and 1987. McPherson was also the DOP for 12 episodes of St. Elsewhere, with four of these episodes featuring one Lance Guest.

Despite the commercial failings of Jaws: The Revenge, McPherson continued to work on big productions including the Amblin Entertainment-produced Batteries Not Included plus Short Circuit 2. From 1989 onwards McPherson also turned his hand to more directing roles, overseeing episodes of Alien Nation, Swamp Thing, The Untouchables, Sliders, Nash Bridges and Beverly Hills 90210.

Another production crew member who carried on working (almost up until this day) was Editor Michael Brown, who began his career as an Assistant Editor for the television series 12 O'Clock High in 1965 would continue to work primarily on the small screen through the 1970s, with the odd exception being Giallo Psychic Killer and 1976's Eaten Alive aka Death Trap, directed by Tobe Hooper, telling the story of a psychotic redneck who fed his victim's bodies to the local crocodile.

Post-Revenge he would continue to work steadily on television movies, with his most recent venture being a Facebook produced mini-documentary series Unfiltered: Paris Jackson and Gabriell Glenn, which follows the launch of Jackson's music career with The Sunflowers duo.

Brown has also turned his hand to screenplays adapting William & Lucy, a romantic story he previously wrote as a book currently in pre-production as of late-2021.

Production Designer John J. Lloyd had carved out a memorable portfolio by the time Jaws: The Revenge came calling in 1987.

He had accumulated a prolific portfolio of television work throughout the 1950s and 60s, with notable work on The Munsters, The Alfred Hitchcock Hour and Theatre of Stars, hosted by legendary entertainer Bob Hope.

Lloyd worked with director John Landis on three films during the 1970s and 1980s, with the creator of An American Werewolf in London having nothing but praise for his work ethic, saying,

"John Lloyd was a terrific man with a great sense of humour. I was lucky to work with him on 'Animal House' 'The Blues Brothers' and 'Into the Night.' John was an old pro and a pleasure to collaborate with."

Lloyd's final production credits include 1988's The Naked Gun, memorably starring Leslie Nielsen and its first sequel The Naked Gun 2 and a Half: The Smell of Fear in 1991.

Donald B. Woodruff's career began as a Set Designer for 1982's western Barbarosa, featuring Willie Nelson and Gary Busey before work on Blue Thunder (starring Roy Scheider), The Goonies and Harry and the Hendersons led to him being hired as Art Director for Jaws: The Revenge.

Woodruff would work steadily in the industry until 2004, with notable credits on films such as The Hunt for Red October, Volcano, Enemy of the State and Pirates of the Caribbean: The Curse of the Black Pearl.

For the second, aerial and underwater units for Jaws: The Revenge, industry experience was the key. Director turned actor James W. Gavin would oversee the aerial unit of the shoot with industry newcomer Lynda Gilman taking on some directing of the second unit. Gilman had previously collaborated with Woodruff on the production of Harry and the Hendersons.

Jordan Klein Sr. was well known for his underwater camera work by the time Revenge hired him to handle their underwater sequences. Klein Sr. has been part of 46 episodes of Flipper plus Jawsploitation Mako: The Jaws of Death (1976), Jaws 3D, Never Say Never Again, Splash and Cocoon. Klein talks more about his experiences working on Jaws IV later in this book.

Another part of the Aerial Unit team was relative newcomer Michelle Marx who had worked on Gloria Estefan's Conga music video and Flight of the Navigator before joining the Revenge crew. Her most notable work post-Jaws was as Production Manager on Adam Sandler vehicle Happy Gilmore and directing some of the Miami section of Bad Boys.

The experienced Wes McAfee was brought on to assist Sargent with the first unit direction having started in the industry in 1958 with war thriller The Naked and the Dead and worked on numerous productions including The Towering Inferno, The Dukes of Hazzard, Magnum P.I and the hit TV series Hawaii Five-O between 1968 and 1977. At 67 years of age, Revenge would be McAfee's penultimate film with his final credit being 1990's The Incident, also directed by Joseph Sargent.

Industry newcomer Stephen Southard was accumulating a steady slew of work on Airwolf, Alfred Hitchcock Presents, Murder She Wrote and Harry and the Hendersons when he joined the crew of Revenge. As previously mentioned, Donald B. Woodruff was Art Director of Hendersons plus a slew of crew members which included Jaws IV producer Frank Baur. Sadly, Southard's career would never reach blockbuster heights as he passed away in 1990 aged just 30.

Ted Swanson was also hired to work on the underwater unit alongside Jordan Klein Sr. for Revenge, having also worked on the second unit of..you guessed it, Harry and the Hendersons the year previous.

Swanson's resume was extremely impressive, with credits on Rocky (1979), Caddyshack (1980) and Witness (1985) starring Harrison Ford. He would continue working up until 2001 with the TV feature Three Blind Mice, based on the novel by Evan Hunter, working as production manager.

Karen Miller Ehrlich cut her teeth as an assistant director on the 1980's Christmas-themed horror Christmas Evil aka You Better Watch Out. After accumulating assistant directing credits on shows such as The Tracey Ullman Show, Ehrlich would join (almost every other member of the Jaws: The Revenge crew!) on Harry and the Hendersons as a Directors Guild of America Trainee. Just a few months later she would join the fourth Jaws film to handle some of the assistant director tasks.

Since Revenge, Ehrlich has worked steadily in television with numerous credits including 2005's Just Shoot Me, Heroes: Destiny in 2008 and long-running sitcom Happy Endings.

The special effects and ultimately, the shark design was split between numerous parties, including two sets of brothers and visual effects gurus who would go on to work in the Marvel Universe and Game of Thrones.

Doug Hubbard had been working in special effects since 1954 but would hit stride in the 1980s with contributions to Weird Science, Commando and again Harry and the Hendersons. Not stunted by his work on Revenge, he would go on to work on blockbusters such as Demolition Man, Face/Off, Starship Troopers and shark thriller Deep Blue Sea.

Dave Hubbard had only previously acted in 1985's Escape Through Time when he joined his sibling for Jaws: The Revenge and hasn't been credited with anything since.

Brothers Mike and Henry Millar would first collaborate on the erotic thriller A Change of Seasons in 1980, before enjoying an extremely busy 1985 with Arnold Schwarznegger's Commando and Weird Science where they would work with Doug Hubbard.

While Mike Millar's final credit was The Naked Gun 2 and a Half: The Smell of Fear (also the final credit of the aforementioned Production Designer John J. Lloyd), Henry would continue working until 1997 with highlights including Last Man Standing (1996) starring Bruce Willis and Sigourney Weaver's Copycat (1995).

The career of special effects technician Michael A. Tice began with Jaws: The Revenge and has gone to the moon and back since, with credits on over 50 productions to date, including numerous Marvel films, Fast & Furious 7, the Transformers series, three Die Hard films and most recently the successful HBO series Lovecraft Country.

Crit Killen was tasked with miniatures (that director Joseph Sargent notoriously disagreed with using) for Jaws 4, having worked on Gremlins, Cocoon, Critters and Big Trouble in Little China. His miniature and visual effects work would be included in many pre-CG productions including Batteries Not Included, The Monster Squad, Beetlejuice, Honey I Shrunk the Kids, Dick Tracy, Alien 3 and Batman Returns.

Ted Rae would be tasked with working on stop motion for Revenge plus the composite for blue screen underwater plates. Rae had previous experience with the Jaws series, having worked on Jaws 3D in 1983 before providing stop motion and visual effects for The Terminator (1984) and The Night of the Comet (1984).

Rae would continue to collaborate with Crit Killen on Beetlejuice whilst also going on to work on A Nightmare on Elm Street 5:

The Dream Child (1989), Babylon 5, Stargate SG1 and Mel Gibson's Apocalypto and The Passion of the Christ. He would land his biggest role to date in 2016 as visual effects supervisor on Game of Thrones whilst also supervising matte photography on the Oscar-winning La La Land in the same year.

Joseph C. Sasgen was another Blue Thunder alumni, having worked on the electronic special effects for the Roy Scheider feature as his third job in the industry. Just a year later in 1984, he would also work on the Lance Guest feature The Last Starfighter before working on Red Dawn, starring Patrick Swayze and Joe Dante's Innerspace before joining the production of Jaws: The Revenge.

Sasgen would continue to work up until 1998, with notable credits including Near Dark (1987), Die Hard 2 and 121 episodes of Star Trek: The Next Generation between 1993 and 1997. His final working credit would be on another Joe Dante production; Small Soldiers.

Roy Scheider Turns Down Return

Roy Scheider's issues with the Jaws series date back to the troubled production of Jaws 2, with the actor seemingly backed into a corner by the studio to return rather than wanting to reprise the role of Martin Brody of his own accord.

Scheider would allegedly spend good chunks of production sunbathing while not mingling with the cast too much. He would also clash with director Jeannot Szwarc (who was brought onto the project following the sacking of John D. Hancock), allegedly leading to a punch-up on-set.

Despite these issues, Scheider would be offered the role of Brody one last time, which he turned down almost immediately.

"We did 'Jaws' once and we did it right," Scheider told the LA Times.

"(Jaws 2 was) contractual obligation that I didn't know I had. I had to do it. Now I don't have to do 'Jaws' anymore. If I'd choose, I could probably continue doing 'Jaws' pictures for the rest of my life, because it seems Universal is going to do 'Jaws' pictures for the rest of their lives. I'm not joining the dance."

With Scheider definitively out of the series, Lorraine Gary would be left to spearhead the Brody's in their latest battle against a killer shark, but who would be joining her this time around?

Return to Amity

Edgartown once again becomes Amity for Jaws: The Revenge

On 2nd February 1987 shooting began in Edgartown, with the target of wrapping the whole shoot (including the Bahamas set pieces) in a mere 54 days.

Reporter Jeanne Wolf would exclusively reveal the first look at the design of the mechanical sharks being transported to the Bahamas on 3rd February, in a short segment on Inside Entertainment for Entertainment Tonight. She would explain how the sharks were being transported via truck cross-country on a special barge purchased by Universal.

At this point, the title of the film was flipping between Jaws '87 and Jaws: The Revenge, with Wolf using both titles during the 30-second segment.

In a feature with the LA Times on 8th February, producer Frank Baur spoke of the pressures of the timeframe being proposed by the studio.

"This will be the fastest I have ever seen a major film planned and executed in all of my 35 years as a production manager," he said.

Sargent was also wary of the fast shoot, calling it a 'ticking time bomb waiting to go off,' despite being only six days into production at this stage.

Despite his worries about the rushed shoot, Sargent was determined to ensure Jaws 4 was completed on time.

"Sid Sheinberg expects a miracle – and we're going to make it happen. If Sid had waited another few weeks, it would have been too late to have made 'Jaws' happen in time for summer."

Sargent said that lessons had been learnt from the previous Jaws films, with regards to the shark design.

"We've learned a lot from 'Jaws 1,' '2' and even '3-D.' But this is the new generation, Bruce. Ours is bigger, more flexible and more realistic looking."

The director was very happy to be working at Martha's Vineyard and praised the locals who had really brought Jaws into their hearts.

"They opened their arms like old relatives had come to visit. This despite the fact we keep bringing sharks back there. Actually, they've staked practically their whole identity on Jaws. They have t-shirts, postcards, inflatable sharks – everything marked Martha's Vineyard or Amity," he told Edward Gross for the August 1987 edition of Fangoria.

For Lorraine Gary, returning to a meatier role as Ellen Brody was something she could only dream of.

"I know I can act. This role is what I used to dream of, until I became happy as a person, no longer depending on acting to be fulfilled," she told Donna Rosenthal in the LA Times.

The actress also spoke candidly about her marriage to Sheinberg and the possible effects it could have had on her career.

"Being married to Sid was a handicap. Some directors were afraid to hire me in case we had disagreements on the set. And I think there are other times that people wouldn't use me because they don't like Sid." And then there were the others, she said, who "would be afraid of appearing to be kissing his behind."

"I made a good deal (on this latest sequel), but I didn't make as good a deal as I would have if I weren't married to Sid,"

She continued,

"This is the one situation where I can genuinely claim to be worth something because I'm not only reprising a role, I'm reprising it for the third time. My deal is very nice, but it's not as nice as Michael Caine's by a long shot. He's a major international star. This is my third time around (as Ellen Brody) and I'm not embarrassed to say I'm getting more because I deserve more, certainly more than I got on Jaws."

It wasn't just Lorraine Gary who would be returning to the Jaws franchise for Revenge, Lee Fierro, who played the mother of Alex Kintner, the shark's second victim in the original film, would return for a brief cameo.

"I appear in the Brody house when one of her sons arrives from the Bahamas with his wife and daughter. We were asked to do a lot of crying," she told journalist Brooks Robards.

"It was absolutely frigid when they were shooting the scene down on the dock. I don't think Hollywood people expected it to be that cold. They were buying out Sundog and Fligors (a local Edgartown delicacy)."

Publisher of the Martha's Vineyard Magazine William Marks also secured the role of the police chief in Amity, who returns Sean Brody's belongings to Ellen post-attack.

"I'm very discreet because I try to return her son's belongings to her, which is obviously inappropriate," he told Robards.

The locals of Edgartown were also given the star treatment by Universal, with the producers organising a party at a local venue for 200 islanders, while also hiring hundreds of extras (250 in total) for scenes that included six handicapped children.

The visit of the Jaws '87 production was a welcome boost to businesses in Edgartown, whose population could drop from 85,000 in the summer to 7000 during the winter.

" 'Jaws' is a welcome relief," Jimmy Carter, owner of the Heritage Hotel, told the LA Times.

"Business in February is always dead, but now three hotels are full thanks to 'Jaws.' A lot of unemployed people are making money too. I didn't like the movie, but I'd welcome a 'Jaws' crew here every year."

Michael Wild was a local production liaison who spent a big chunk of time tracking down summer residents and asking for their permission to park trucks on their drives and put up Christmas lights, with the film being set around the festive period.

"I've been sending letters and cables to all the sunny spots trying to track down the residents," Wild said.

"I even sent one cable to a lady who's in Bombay to get permission to turn on the lights outside her house."

Director of Photography John McPherson described the shoots in Martha's Vineyard as the most challenging.

"We were shooting only six days and did 11 pages (of the script)," he told American Cinematographer for their August 1987 issue.

"It was bitterly cold – about 10 degrees Fahrenheit, and everything locked up for the winter. Therefore, we couldn't use any practicals for the night shots. We lit using everything. It required seven generators and a lot of equipment."

Mitchell Anderson (Sean Brody) was interviewed by William Rus for the documentary Behind the Scenes of Jaws: The Revenge (which would screen on 10th July 1987) on the first night of shooting his attack scene in Edgartown harbour.

"Tonight the shark comes up and bites off my arm, so they are shredding my arm and putting a lot of blood on me and I will be screaming, hollering and yelling to the people on shore" Anderson told Rus.

"It is a little segment but will take about four hours and about three and half seconds on the screen," he joked.

"Every time they do the effect something new happens and you are kind of looking into the dark water and all of a sudden a big explosion happens and fish comes out and it is pretty scary."

Joseph Sargent also weighed on the scene, saying,

"It has taken somewhere in the vicinity of seven underwater special effects men with their scuba outfits to set up all of the motion with the boat rocking and showing the effects of Jaws attacking the boat."

What the production didn't count on was the snowstorms that blanketed Martha's Vineyard for the best part of a month, providing an icy backdrop for the filming of *Revenge*.

Cameras would roll on a variety of quaintly named areas such as sections of Edgartown, Gazette, the fantastically named Chappaquiddick and East Chop.

In the aftermath of Sean Brody's death, a local gravestone maker from Edgartown was hired to turn out 51 slabs to lend some authenticity to the funeral sequence. This scene would also require plenty of Edgartown extras, as Amity mourns the loss of another Brody.

With six days of intense shooting in the bag, the production of Jaws: The Revenge would now be relocating to the sunnier shores of Nassau.

Bahamas Bound

Jordan Klein Sr. filming the infamous Banana Boat attack scene

The Bahamas had a rich history with Hollywood before the Jaws crew rolled into town. Most notably, the Bond series used the region, starting with Thunderball in 1965, You Only Live Twice (1967), The Spy Who Loved Me (1977) Moonraker (1979), For Your Eyes Only (1981), and Never Say Never Again (1983). In a slight Jaws connection, The Island was also filmed in Antigua and Abaco. Based on the novel by Jaws scribe Peter Benchley, The Island was produced by Jaws and Jaws 2 alumni David Brown and Richard D. Zanuck and featured Jaws: The Revenge star Michael Caine.

On 9th February 1987 the production of Revenge would move to Nassau in the Bahamas, with principal photography starting the following day. The filming of Jaws: The Revenge would continue here until 2nd April. Principal photography was completed on 26th May, despite Henry Millar's team remaining in Nassau until 4th June, just a handful of weeks before the 17th July release date.

While the crew were hoping for a tropical paradise for filming, they were greeted with troubled waters and storm clouds. The production crew quickly realised this was not going to be the smooth shoot they had envisioned and began making plans for times when the weather made filming impossible outdoors. This would include cover shots on shore when the weather was foul at sea plus a third plan where interior 'cover sets' were employed when the weather on-shore made filming problematic and unsafe.

Heading up the Special Effects was the experienced Millar, whose ultimate responsibility was operating the sharks that were all based at South Beach, Nassau. *Revenge* would start utilising these models (one of 7 constructed) on 10th March 1987.

The shark was to be launched from atop an 88 foot long platform which had been purposely built ashore and floated out to the middle of Clifton Bay. This platform was made from the trussed turret of a 30 foot crane with two additional cranes (a 145 ton and 110 ton) required to lift the apparatus into the channel from where it was to be towed into the Bay.

The platform was capable of rotating 180 degrees under water and was also rigged with a hydraulically operated arm that could turn the shark 260 degrees.

The issue was being able to mount the shark on that arm atop a buoyant platform that was being buffeted about by chopping seas.

The shark was actually seven sharks or segments thereof. Two models were fully articulated, two were made for jumping, one for ramming, one was a half shark (the top half) and one was just a fin. The two fully articulated models each had 22 sectioned ribs and moveable jaws covered by a flexible water-based latex skin, measured 25 feet in length and weighed 2500 pounds.

Each tooth was half a foot long and as sharp as it looked. All of the aforementioned models were housed under cover of a 40 by 80 foot tent based at a secret location in Nassau.

Lorraine Gary was subject to a very cynical article in the 4th February edition of The Indianapolis Star where gossip column Liz Smith's Gossip claimed Sid Sheinberg had given Gary the lead role in Jaws: The Revenge as a Christmas present.

"Not every man can give his wife just what she wants. But at Christmas, movie tycoon Sid Sheinberg did just that. He wrapped up the screenplay currently titled 'Jaws 87' for his actress-mate Lorraine Gary, promising she'll get to reprise her original 1975 role as the wife in a small New England resort.

"What's more, in this sequel to the sequels, Lorraine not only will co-star with the great white shark; she'll also get to kill it in a violent episode of woman vs nature," Smith said.

The 17th March edition of the Wausau Daily Herald carried an interview with actress Karen Young, who was still filming as Carla Brody (wife of Michael Brody) in Jaws: The Revenge.

"I play a welder-sculptor married to one of the boys from the original, who is now grown-up," she said.

"This time there is more emphasis on the people than the shark."

Young also noted that the filmmakers were taking advantage of the advances in technology since the original Jaws, to make the most realistic version of a shark to date.

Journalists Roderick Barrand and Colin Dongaard spoke to Michael Caine, whilst still filming in Nassau, about why he chose to work on Jaws: The Revenge.

"Because of my daughter, I've got a 13-year old Natasha. She and her friends won't' go and see my other pictures like 'Educating Rita' and 'Hannah and Her Sisters', that stuff's boring to them," Caine said.

"But they'll go and see this one alright, this one will knock their socks off!"

"Apart from wanting to make a picture for Natasha, every now and then I must do what I call 'my bit of fun'" Caine noted.

"I'm playing a bloke who flies around the islands all day, a salty character like Bob (Robert) Shaw's in the first Jaws. I love the script, I call it a personal horror picture. The shark is a terror that could exist, it's not like some great monster coming out of a swamp."

Journalist Donna Rosenthal continued her coverage of the production of Jaws: The Revenge, with a visit to the Bahamas set in Nassau for a report in the 22nd March edition of The Daily News.

Rosenthal reported that Revenge was aiming for a 3rd July release date, but the crew were battling against challenging weather plus the mechanical failings of the sharks.

Speaking on-set Michael Caine told her,

"This Jaws is different, the plot is gripping, the characters compelling, and the shark much more realistic. Jaws 2 and Jaws 3-D were so awful – I was rooting for the shark."

Nassau was a different animal to Martha's Vineyard, with the millions pumped into their economy barely noticed, given it was heaving with tourists before the crew arrived. An unnamed Bahamas politician told Rosenthal,

"The biggest business here is cocaine. There are more sharks in our government making a fortune from cocaine than in Jaws."

The Bahamian government was said to be very sensitive about its image and requested Mario Van Peebles not wear a wig with dreadlocks as they said he would be confused with a Rastafarian who smokes marijuana.

Van Peebles argued the case with the Tourist Commission and won and thus kept his dreadlocks.

Universal created an 'authentic' Bahamian village of wood huts, shipped in 18 tonnes of sand to the beach and also constructed a pier (at the sea-front of Michael Brody's house) at the cost of $150,000.

Four complete models of Bruce 4 (as he was coined) were constructed for the Nassau shoot, all 25 feet in length. Each model weighed over a tonne and was constructed of fibreglass over a metal frame and latex skin.

Rosenthal also revealed that once filming was complete in the Bahamas, the models would be shipped to the Universal Pictures tank for further filming.

Edward Gross, a journalist for Fangoria and Starlog, visited the final day of shooting on the Nassau set for coverage in their August issues respectively.

Joseph Sargent told Gross how Revenge was going to be different from the previous sequels, given how it has the emotional core of Ellen Brody's journey as its driving force.

"At first mention of Jaws 3, 4 or whatever, you tend to feel like you're dealing with used clothing. But this movie is such a departure from the two previous Jaws in that we're dealing with more of an emotional base where you can easily empathise with the characters, which is why we've all responded so enthusiastically," he said.

"We had very little to go on, to begin with, so we began to pile 'bricks' one on top of each other until all of these disconnected elements began to take on a form and a shape. Pretty soon, the piece's emotional content began to solidify, and before we knew it, we had a very interesting clothesline on which to hang all of these elements. Originally, we started with nothing more than the death of Sheriff Martin Brody, since we knew Roy Scheider couldn't do the picture due to another commitment. So, we focused on Ellen Brody and her feeling that the shark, in effect, had a vendetta against the family, thereby introducing a whole mystical aspect to the shark."

Sargent was keen to continue the narrative that Jaws: The Revenge was the 'pure' Jaws 2, discarding the previous two sequels.

"I would tend to hope that people look at the film that way," he said.

"Although, there were excellent moments in Jaws 2 in the fact that it furthered the Brody's family growth. The boys were a little older, and the family (was) more firmly established. This is almost a very short mini-series where we take the characters a few years down the road."

In full-publicity mode, Sargent also teased what audiences could expect from the finished film, saying,

"With Jaws the Revenge the audience can expect a much more terrifying and more spectacular shark doing rather spectacular things, and they can expect a very identifiable and heartwarming emotional story since it deals with a woman whose whole family seems to be deteriorating and her obsessive belief that there is a vendetta against them on the part of the great white shark."

Sargent also discussed the decision to go with a mechanical shark, instead of a repurposed humpback whale used in Star Trek IV.

"It became so problematic and expensive because it's one-third scale, which meant we'd have to scale down our people. It probably would have been a bit disconcerting to have our principals replaced by three-foot people during key scenes," he explained.

The director was glad the production decided to go with the mechanical sharks instead, saying,

"Ours is a much more sophisticated replica of a shark's articulation in the wiggle, the tail and surprisingly enough; the gums. As a shark's mouth opens to devour its prey, a drop of the gums takes place and the engineers have included that in our model. So you will swear that we trained and developed our own shark. He's going to be rather special."

Gross also spoke to writer Michael De Guzman, who was also on-set in Nassau.

"By the end of October (1986), we had (the) bare bones of a story. By 2nd November, we had an outline for the pre-production people. By mid-December, we had the first draft, by mid-January a shooting script. The writing has continued throughout production. We're six months into it. Whereas other major releases might still be on their second draft during this same time span," De Guzman explained.

"I tell people that this story is about obsession and fear. Whether what Ellen Brody has in her mind is true or not will be left up to the audience to decide. No statement is being made in that regard. I don't want to get into that, but in a larger more general sense, it is about any kind of fear so great and so strong that it begins to take control of a human being's life, and the ultimate knowledge that in order to get on in life, fear must be confronted."

Cinematographer John McPherson also supervised principal photography plus the 15-man special underwater unit which boasted a combined 230 years of underwater filming experience.

Speaking on-set in Nassau, McPherson told American Cinematographer magazine about the importance of being able to bring his Hollywood crew to the set, saying,

"Work with people long enough and they know how you think. I like to see people being creative in their own right, but when it's time to shift gears and go faster these guys are not offended when you ask them to.

Underwater cinematography was completed by Pete Romano, who used Arriflex cameras equipped with Zeiss Superspeed lenses and centered for Super 35. Romano teamed up with experienced underwater photographers Wayne Baker and Jack McKinney for the shoot.

Sargent also spoke to American Cinematographer about his frustrations with the mechanical sharks.

"We're fighting so many elements here it's becoming embarrassing. Five sharks are under repair."

When filming the sequence where Hoagie crashlands the plane, the crew required a second plane after the first one sank to the bottom of the ocean. Ironically, the plane is still there in Nassau and has been photographed by many scuba divers in the intervening years.

"We're now using another airplane like it, with floatation foam to keep it at a proper level for each scene," Sargent added.

McPherson also spoke of his delight in working with Sargent.

"Joe's a great director to work with. His excitement and enthusiasm help us all, and he can make light of adverse situations that would drive some directors crazy. We bounce ideas off each other and he gives me a tremendous amount of freedom," McPherson said.

"It's good when you work with a director who shares his vision with you and allows you to implement your thoughts onto what he's expressed to you."

McPherson also talked about his decision to use the Super 35 format for filming.

"Our cameras were centred by Panavision to Super 35 specifications. We're doing our blue screen work in Vista Vision. Everybody wanted to shoot anamorphic but me. I finally talked them out of it, partly because I don't like anamorphic lenses. Panavision does have some wonderful new anamorphic lenses, but generally speaking, I don't like the squeezed look anamorphic gives you – spherical lenses are much superior. Also, the underwater photography would have been a bit cumbersome due to the heaviness of the anamorphic lenses. We decided to consider shooting it in other formats and I felt it might be nice to shoot in Super 35 and have one wonderful lens at the laboratory do all the anamorphic work for the consistency of the same look and colour. I had tested Super 35 before, but hadn't shot it before."

McPherson also chatted about the challenges of lighting in the tropical location of Nassau.

"I was really in a quandary about how to approach certain shots. Like a lot of cinematographers, I love a really pretty backlight or sidelight. But for one thing, the beautiful colours and textures we had available to us were rendered only in frontlight. There were miles and miles of water only 10 to 20 feet deep, and it would reflect such gorgeous colour. Beyond that was a 6000-foot drop-off, so that the water became almost black. Against that little bit of blackness was that deep, deep blue sky above and those great billowing clouds. Also, we had black actors who looked great in frontlight. That is the opposite of what I like to do," he said.

"So, there are two different looks in the Bahamas scenes; the frontlight with all the spectacular colours, and a backlight condition where the figures go toward silhouette a lot. I used hazed filters sometimes when the air was a little murky, to cut through the ultra violet.

The unpredictable weather in Nassau would also mean that some scenes were filmed across a number of days.

"The weather changed every single day, and some scenes had to be continued over two or more days. We were always concerned about matching, sometimes the scenes were sunny, some days were heavily overcast. Sometimes it would change during a shot. I was always debating with myself how long we could wait, and sometimes we couldn't wait any longer," McPherson mused.

The final shot of the film was originally going to show the impaled shark spiraling down to the bottom of the ocean away from the camera. After an initial test Sargent decided the shot would not work and abandoned the idea.

Little Buddy Productions, who were contracted to produce stop motion miniatures for *Revenge*, conducted a second test to attempt to add more blood coming from the shark's mouth and more bubbles but it took Sargent four days to say he was still unsatisfied with the results.

Ted Rae, who was part of Little Buddy Productions, told Cinefantastique in March 1988, that the reason for the shot not working was because Sargent (potentially pushed for time, having gone over schedule) approved the storyboard so quickly.

To achieve the desired shot, Sargent had the Universal sound stage 23 refilled with water, at a cost of $25,000 and spent two days shooting the redesigned scene. Although there were no contractual obligations, Little Buddy turned over their miniatures to Universal, wanting to be good sports to the production.

Rae told Cinefantastique,

"It was exasperating to see Tim's mechanism, which took five weeks to build, completely trashed in one day's shooting."

On 10th July 1987, a week before the film's cinematic release a documentary, 'Behind the Scenes of Jaws: The Revenge' was released on WSBK-TV with behind the scenes footage and interviews with the cast.

Director William Rus quizzed a number of the cast about why man has this fear of sharks, with Michael Caine saying,

"This is a monster that you could very easily meet, I mean you are hardly ever likely to meet Frankenstein's monster or any of those creepy monster things; but Jaws you could," when asked about the human fascination with sharks.

"We just have a fascination with animals that can eat us," weighed in Mario Van Peebles.

Lorraine Gary added,

"The sharks are every demon we cannot conquer."

Lance Guest commented,

"They are top of the food chain and nobody messes with a great white."

Rus focused on the character of Ellen Brody and quizzed Gary about her character's motivations in this film.

"Ellen has inherited the family obsession from Martin, her husband, who firmly believed that there was a shark stalking, first the island of Amity and secondly the Brody family and Ellen feels that it is the Brody fate that the shark will yet again strike," she said.

Explaining the character of Hoagie, Caine said,

"He's not a shark hunter, he's a pilot. He's a sort of stock Hollywood character which I haven't played many. He is the old guy who knows everything.

Talking about signing onto *Revenge* he also added,

"It's gone back to human beings as I believe you can't get to terror in a film unless you've got believable people."

Second Unit Director Jordan Klein spoke about directing the underwater sequences in Nassau.

"They are in a foreign environment. They have been told a couple of times what to expect, what we're going to and what the scenes are and then they get down there and all of these things are happening. There are a lot of people surrounding them and suddenly their brains go up in locks until they've done it (the scene) a few times," he said.

Mario Van Peebles also told Rus about his experiences of underwater filming, saying,

"It's weird you go down underwater and there's a guy checking your face and there is another guy doing the clipboard and the cameraman. It's just everybody's in a wetsuit underwater; it's just a completely (different) thing. We had to get our hand signals down, to indicate doing another take, stop, close-up because you can't speak. Once you get your hand signals down and get comfortable underwater it's not that tough."

All of the underwater sequences were coordinated from an 85-foot boat called Moby II.

"The Moby II is our platform, totally self-sufficient. We have our own compressor, we have dive equipment, camera equipment, lighting equipment and just generally everything needed to complete the second unit of underwater work here," Klein added.

The second unit director also discussed the scene involving the moray eel which startled Michael during his first trip back into the ocean post-attack.

"When we turn them loose we have no idea which way he was going to go; whether it's at the camera, to the bottom or at the diver's throats. So Gavin (McKinney) who is doubling for Lance (Guest) to do the shot, is told about the scene beforehand and the risks involved," Klein said.

Cameraman Pete Romano also commented,

"If they (the moray eel) latch onto you with their jaws, you are supposed to have to kill them to get them off, so we were sort of concerned about that so we ended up with Jordan Klein holding the eel by the neck and would throw him into the camera and we would retrieve him with a net before doing the shot over and over again.

Doctor John McCosker was brought into the production as a consultant, to attempt to portray the shark's behaviour as accurately as possible. McCosker was noted as having studied the behaviour of great white sharks across the coast of California and Australia.

"No one knows how many white sharks there are, we guess there are hundreds, possibly thousands of them across the California coast but the fact they are so uncommon is what makes it so frightening," he told Rus.

The documentary also focuses on the infamous banana boat attack scene, which was split in half; with the on-shore portion filmed first.

Karen Young (Carla Brody) spoke briefly about filming the scene,

"I hear her (Thea's) grandmother screaming her name and I look over and see her and where she is looking and I see the (shark) fin and I have to run into the water and save her," she said.

Lynn Whitfield also added,

"It's like the classic kind of Trojan women thing with all the women there and screaming to save another woman's child. It's the women against the shark."

In preparation for the move to the underwater part of the sequence, the shark's assault is mapped out. The banana boat sequence was considered the most difficult to shoot primarily because there were children on the inflatable which was being pulled by a high-speed boat that was going at quite a high speed.

There were other boats on the water, with people enjoying themselves who would be abruptly interrupted by a 4000-pound shark set to cause chaos.

Stunt actress Dianne Hatfield, who played the mother devoured by the shark, was quite excited about filming the sequence.

"When we saw the fin of the shark coming, we all started screaming as we knew Jaws was coming. We were all holding onto each other and screaming."

The challenge of the scene was achieving the technical logistics of the scene coupled with the gut-wrenching horror of the attack.

Sargent was quite ambiguous when quizzed on the film's title, telling Gus that he wanted audiences to decide whether they were seeing the revenge of the shark or Ellen Brody.

"It's almost a psychological story of obsession and denial and courage on everyone's part," said Gary.

For the film's closing sequence the production spent a number of days filming in the unpredictable Bahamian waters.

"The biggest difficulty of filming at sea is that nothing stays in the frame too long," Sargent told Rus.

"I have a shot setup but by the time the lights are all set up and adjustments are made and the actors are ready and we've rehearsed; everything has drifted completely out of range."

During filming Mario Van Peebles received a call from the Make a Wish Foundation on behalf of a boy who was dying of cancer who wanted to meet one of the cast members.

He shared this heartfelt anecdote in the January 1995 edition of Starlog,

"He was a super bright kid who had done extensive reading on the great white shark," Van Peebles recalled.

"His father was a diver and the kid would go diving with him before he was diagnosed as having cancer. Having seen Jaws, one of his biggest fears was that the shark would get him. He knew he was dying, but he became fascinated with the shark. As I wondered why, it became clear to me that what he was making peace with death; the scariest thing he could face was death, and this was the scariest thing any diver would ever face, especially from this little boy's perspective. He was making peace with the scariest monster he could, by understanding it, by getting into its mind."

With as much filming completed in Nassau as possible, the concluding jigsaw pieces of Jaws: The Revenge would be added on the Universal backlot.

Filming at Universal

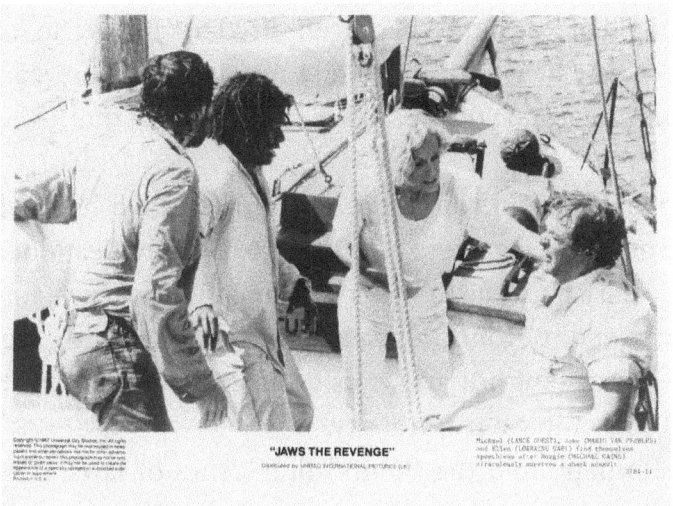

Hoagie escapes the shark aboard Neptune's Folly

As previously alluded to in the first production chapter, director Joseph Sargent requested for two sets to be built on the Universal backlot with the aim of getting a more cinematic effect without worrying about the hydraulics of the shark failing in the unpredictable waters of Edgartown or Nassau.

The crew would arrive at Universal on 2nd April, not knowing that filming there would not be complete until after the film had been released theatrically.

The first set, a 30 foot deep sound stage indoors, was filled with over a million gallons of water, with the first sequence filmed being the shipwreck chase with Michael and the shark.

Whitey Krumm who had previously worked as a special effects coordinator on Airwolf was put in charge of the mechanical sharks, taking the reigns from John McPherson.

In his book My Life as a Mankiewicz: An Insider's Journey Through Hollywood, Tom Mankiewicz recalls an amusing story of Krumm being fired from The Naked Gun for failing to blow up a car six times. Mankiewicz walked out of his bungalow one morning and ran into Sargent, who learned that Krumm had been fired and in the couple of days since had been hired for Jaws: The Revenge.

"Joe, maybe he is good at sharks. You don't have any cars to blow up in your movie, do you, because he's not good at that," Mankiewicz mused.

Renowned production designer John J. Lloyd had painted the tank bottom the near-white colour of the Bahama seafloor and simulated the dark patterns that mark the locations of coral formations. At the east end, beyond the weir that kept water flowing and the illusion of a distant horizon, was a huge cyclorama that had been painted to resemble a tropical sky.

Pete Romano told the Behind the Scenes of Jaws: the Revenge documentary,

"The tanks allow for a more controlled environment where you can control your lighting. It's easier to communicate with your people and there were so many complicated things that all needed to happen at once that this was the place to do it."

Outside at Universal, a crew of 75 constructed the second set which was another double of the Bahamas, which would house a 3 million gallon tank of water for the final confrontation between the shark and the Brody's, Jake and Hoagie. The location known as Falls Lake was formerly based near the infamous Bates Motel house from the Psycho movies and has been in use since 1926. The skyline for Falls Lake was designed specifically for the production of *Revenge* and it would go on to be used in countless Universal productions including The Lost World, Pirates of the Caribbean 4 and Dunkirk.

This tank took 24 hours to fill, which was at the time, the largest tank in Hollywood. Artwork crews were then brought into designing matte paintings to resemble a Bahamas backdrop and sky using several shades of blue paint.

Instead of the barge used for filming in Nassau, four cameras were mounted onshore and on huge cranes that would reach across the lake. Technician Rick Thompson revealed that there were five actuators inside the shark being used for the climactic scene. Special effects men would be based underwater and would pump barrels of blood to the shark, which would be regurgitated as it was impaled and killed.

The model of Neptune's Folly designed by Little Buddy Productions – photo credit Diana Hamman

Thompson also revealed how the model of Neptune's Folly was designed to disintegrate coupled with the shark model spewing fake blood everywhere which would stain the water, making any reshoots even more time consuming as it would take time to get the water looking clear again.

Dyes were also being used on the water, to attempt to mirror the colour of the Caribbean. An unsubstantiated rumour said that the dye which was eventually chosen actually dyed Lorraine Gary and Michael Caine's hair green.

Speaking at the Universal backlot, Caine discussed the finale,

"What happens in a movie is like if you get wet you get out, but now I got wet in the Bahamas and I am now getting wet in some very cold water here. Weeks later they are still pouring water over you because you were wet in the scenes. The big difference here is to try and keep the dye out of your hair," he joked.

An 11,000-pound boat (doubling Neptune's Folly) was lowered into the water and prepared for destruction.

Lorraine Gary, when interviewed for the behind-the-scenes documentary actually minorly spoils the ending for viewers, saying,

"At the climax of the movie Ellen, Michael and Hoagie are on the boat and dealing with the shark and the shark and the boat collide in a way that I can't reveal to you."

McPherson also weighed in on the use of the Universal backlot tank as an alternative filming location plus the pressures the crew were under to deliver the film by July 1987 -

"The backdrop was made of a material with flaws that became very prominent in the mornings until about 10 am and again in the afternoon around 3:30. Although we tried to keep it out of focus, it almost lent itself to being a wall instead of a sky. Everybody was aware of it, but this film was under the gun, time-wise, from the get-go. They wanted it in the marketplace on 4th July, and as we are sitting here today, 5th June, it's going to be in theatres on 17th July. It's a really fast turn around and everybody was scurrying about to make things work," he said.

It was Joe Sargent's decision to employ a slow-motion technique for the last sequence, with McPherson believing that the more articulated models being used on *Revenge* would help to match the three filming locations shot together in the editing room.

"Joe thought that slow motion to quick cutting would be beneficial to the moves of the shark at certain times. Out of necessity sometimes comes art," he said.

The death of Sean Brody at the start of the film was also part of this shoot, with extra shots filmed where Sean falls out of the boat and holds onto the barge for dear life. Actor Mitchell Anderson was called back to film those sequences in an indoor tank.

Anderson recalled filming at Universal and another accident involving a sinking form of transport...

"They had a replica of the boat on hydraulics in the middle of this huge pool. We were shooting my close up POV shots as the shark attacked the boat and took my arm, finally pulling me under the water. The hydraulics were to shake and roll the boat as it was getting attacked. At one point, I was out there alone on the boat waiting while they set up a shot, and I heard this crash. The boat had fallen off the rack. I called out to the crew on the other side of the pool, 'Uh guys? I think I'm sinking.' They laughed and said I was just being dramatic. But sure enough, two minutes later, the boat sank to the bottom of the tank and I swam to the side," Anderson said.

Lance Guest was one of the first crew members to be informed of the decision to reshoot the film's ending, just a few days after the film's US release.

The initial plan was to re-shoot in Malibu as this was where Mario Van Peebles lived, but it was eventually decided that the Universal backlot would suffice.

Speaking to Pat Jankiewicz in Just When You Thought It Was Safe: A Jaws Companion, Guest explained,

"We wound up shooting it in a tank instead of Malibu, where Mario Van Peebles lived, after the shark got him. In a strange way, it was just like another day at the office when we did it, because we had spent the last month and a half shooting in that tank (on the Universal backlot), now we were back and re-shooting four days *after* the movie came out!"

Sid Sheinberg stated in the Jaws: The Revenge official soundtrack booklet that, 'the only thing wrong with the film is the ending. The impact of the shark dying and Mario (Van Peebles) dying was too much for the audience in one finale.'

Additional footage was now needed to ensure Jake's survival and this coupled with some special effects footage (including the use of miniatures which Sargent strongly objected to) saw the shark inexplicably explode after being speared by the boat. This would be added to the international release of *Revenge* and explains why some countries would see a completely different and quite frankly, less cohesive conclusion than US cinemagoers.

Ted Rae from Little Buddy Productions, as previously alluded to, worked on the miniatures, which were brought to the Universal backlot shoot on the insistence of Sargent to be used in tweaking the finale.

Rae was commissioned to create a mechanical shark for the finale, where the shark is impaled by the boat and sinks to the bottom of the sea. From a design by Tim Lawrence, this model would simulate death spasms of the shark as it drifted out of shot. Rae would also tweak this model so it resembled the mechanical version of the shark more closely. He initially filmed the shot dry for wet using smoke for diffusion with the camera pointing straight up to the shark mounted on a rod that ascended to the roof. He dumped small plastic beads for bubbles and red tempera powder to double as blood, which could be seen floating to the surface in an overhead shot.

When Sargent saw these shots he immediately pulled the plug on them and took the miniatures over to the Universal backlot where they would be filmed in the water tank instead.

Rae had become increasingly frustrated at this stage, telling Cinefantastique in September 1987,

"The production was so far behind it was like pulling teeth to get answers out of anybody. I was almost operating in a vacuum, making stuff up and hoping they would like it. They got caught up in trying to make a movie in 9 months that should have had 18 months."

From Script to Screen

The final draft of the script for Jaws: The Revenge is dated 23rd January 1987, just 9 days before shooting would actually begin in Edgartown, for the Amity scenes.

Here we will analyse the script from Michael De Guzman and highlight areas that were excluded or included/extended in the finished film.

The initial dialogue between Ellen and Sean in the kitchen is trimmed down, with Ellen referring to the deceased Brody being faster than a rabbit making love when talking about her son who also has a penchant for swiping food.

We find out that it is the next day when Ellen, Sean and Tiffany are walking through the very festive streets of Amity discussing the Christmas decorations.

Ellen and Mrs Taft get slightly more dialogue as she leaves work for the night, accompanied by her son and his fiance. It is also revealed that Ellen works in Real Estate, in partnership with Agnes Taft with their firm called 'Brody and Taft Real Estate'.

As they cross the street we briefly get to meet the Mayor, who is simply referred to as Jim, who offers Ellen to come over on Thursday night for a glass of Eggnog.

Talking with Tiffany, Ellen mentions that Sean has the messiest room in America, which alludes to him still living at home, something we suspected in the film but was never 100% confirmed.

If the timeline is correct to the present day, the plaque for Martin Brody's portrait in the Amity Police Station reads that he retired as Police Chief in 1985, and has since passed away in the intervening two years.

Some of the dialogue from Sean to Tarkanian (the choirmaster) on the docks looks to have been added whilst filming as it is not present here, mainly the line about the choir being better than when Sean was a shepherd being absent.

The attack of Sean is certainly more graphic on-screen, again with Mitchell Anderson's guttural screams really adding to the savage nature of the assault.

For the identification of the body, we get more dialogue from Lenny about there not being enough for a positive identification before guiding Ellen into the morgue area. In the script, Ellen also accepts Lenny's offer of Sean's belongings, whereas in the film she leaves promptly and distraught after seeing the remains.

Once Michael and his family arrive in Amity, we get a brief scene between Michael and Carla where they talk about Sean and how his older brother gave him his first drink. While this could be considered filler, it could have been a nice few seconds showing a closer bond between the brothers, which feels oddly lacking in the finished film, especially given how they only briefly share the one scene over the telephone.

Ellen has some slightly amended dialogue when she is arguing with Michael about changing jobs. Instead of saying,

'He died from fear. The fear of it killed him', referring to Brody, she says 'He died from fear...From having to go out there after it...' – which feels a bit clunkier.

The next day as Michael and Carla are walking across the beach, Michael talks about Sean's good nature, before voicing his frustrations to his wife.

Another difference from the final shoot had Carla chase after Michael as he unexpectedly starts running down the beach.

A deleted scene post-Sean's funeral sees Ellen walk down to the shoreline and fire the final six bullets from his service revolver into the sea. This scene was included in the novelisation, with the shark sensing her presence and heading in her direction before she got out of the water.

Michael and Carla suggest that Ellen come back with them to the Bahamas, with the widow instinctively saying yes almost immediately. In the script, she also says in closing,

"I need to be away from here."

On the plane ride to Nassau, after Carla talks about how she always wanted to ride on the back of a boat in a parachute, Thea also chimes in to say she'd like to try it too. This amuses Carla, as she states the daredevil likeness between father and daughter.

Michael alludes to Hoagie's wild side on the plane ride over as he gets to know Ellen.

On the taxi ride to the Brody household, Carla also reiterates to Ellen about relaxing and not waiting on them hand and foot. Michael also points out Neptune's Folly, his boat as they pass it, foreshadowing its importance later on. Ellen reveals in passing that her uncle taught her to sail, which again seems like very obvious foreshadowing.

Carla and Ellen have a brief interaction before getting into the house where Ellen shouts Thea down from the rope swing on the dock.

The dialogue from Thea about the neighbourhood children playing on the dock also looks to have been added in whilst filming.

We meet Jake on board the barge, and the exchanges between him and Michael are slightly extended and certainly benefit from some trimming in the final cut.

Carla discusses her sculpture with Ellen as the grandmother cleans the windows, in an act of defiance from their earlier conversation. This scene feels again like filler and doesn't really add anything to the overall plot.

Once back onboard Jake and Michael briefly argue about his results before the conversation descends into talk of beer with shipmates Clarence and William as the foursome celebrate another day's work.

On Christmas Day, Ellen alludes to more mischievous shenanigans from a childhood Michael before the conversation is halted by Thea mentioning the deceased Sean.

During this exchange, we find out that Jake and Louisa aren't married yet, a fact Jake makes light of.

Ellen begins to walk off to the window as the phone rings, with Thea answering the call of one Matt Hooper. Thea mistakes him for her deceased uncle before Michael takes the phone and Hooper apologises for the mistaken identity and offers his condolences for Sean's death.

This telephone exchange continues across a few pages, with Michael asking Hooper to talk some sense into Ellen about her theory of the shark curse.

Hooper also talks about the Christmas he spent with the Brodies in the Bahamas and discusses Michael's degree. Martin Brody was also present for this Christmas party in the past, dressing as Santa Claus for Thea.

The fascinating thing about this sequence, given it is present in the final shooting script is the assumption that Universal must have been confident they could secure Richard Dreyfuss for a cameo (or recast the role) despite Roy Scheider's aversion to returning.

Ellen's first 'sense' of the shark is led by dialogue (mainly to herself) instead of a musical cue like in the finished film.

Michael and Jake discuss future funding options in more detail, with the conversation descending into Jake criticising William and Clarence for their lack of ambition.

After deciding on a plane ride with Hoagie, Ellen is regaled on the plane with two of Hoagie's 'tales' before being prompted to take the wheel.

Once they arrive at their destination Ellen sees Hoagie meeting a mysterious man, who he hands a bulging envelope, hinting at

Hoagie's backstory as an undercover detective, masquerading as a pilot which plays a big role in Hank Searls' novelisation.

When Ellen and Hoagie arrive back at the Brody house, it is hinted that Hoagie wants more than a handshake but is shut down on this occasion.

At the casino, Jake and Louisa spar playfully again about getting married as Michael becomes unsettled by Hoagie's presence at the table for Louisa's party.

Michael cuts in on Hoagie and Ellen on the dancefloor, with Ellen's speech about moving on a bit extended, with her stating that she will stay one more week before returning to Amity.

The most amusing part of the script is that the line from Michael about making love to an angry welder was actually written by De Guzman and not ad-libbed by Guest when filming.

Hoagie and Ellen's 'date' is slightly extended with more dialogue from Hoagie asking her to stay in the Bahamas longer.

During the imitation scene with Thea and Michael at the dinner table, Thea breaks the silence by mentioning how her Uncle Sean used to make funny faces at her. It does seem that Sean Brody, while not physically being in many scenes, is present through others more in the script than the actual finished film.

Once Thea has gone to bed Ellen tries to get through to Michael, but instead, this turns into a mini-rant from Michael about the same shark not killing his father and brother after Ellen mentions he looks like Brody after the first shark came to Amity. Interestingly, Ellen mentions the first shark, despite Jaws: The Revenge aimed as a direct sequel to the original, thus erasing Jaws 2, where another shark attacks Amity.

Michael has the nightmare about the shark attacking him but in the same scene, Ellen also wakes up startled by what seems like the same dream, which points to a connection between Michael as well as Ellen and the shark.

The next day as Michael is searching for conch, Clarence sees the shark first, as its fin breaches the surface, in what would have been a great visual sequence, before descending to attack Michael in the submersible.

Following the attack in the shipwreck, when Michael decides to go back diving (getting back on the horse, as he says), the dialogue in the script is slightly reduced, with Jake more concerned about them missing Carla's gig than Michael putting himself in harm's way again.

Back on the beach, Louisa has slightly more dialogue about wanting to go on the banana boat with Thea, as Carla waits for her presentation.

After the banana boat attack, we see Ellen take Neptune's Folly, while Michael and Jake can be heard singing and drinking on the porch of Jake's home nearby, oblivious to their boat being 'borrowed'. This scene ends with Michael and Jake arguing over Jake singing about a shark, which Michael feels is in poor taste.

Once Michael and Jake team up with Hoagie, Michael tells them his mother doesn't need a drug dealer as a boyfriend, which is laughed off by the pilot.

Ellen, when she senses the shark is stalking the boat, has a little more dialogue, saying,

"Come and get me you son of a bitch. Take me and leave my family alone…"

This is another instance where the single line works better in the film because it tells us enough without feeling clunky and unnecessary.

Michael suggests that it should be him who attempts to put the electrical device in the shark's mouth and not Jake, saying it is his fault it is coming for them.

When the shark does breach it actually comes for Michael first, then it seems to change trajectory in mid-air and bite down on Jake and the bowsprit, swallowing the device in the process.

Once the shark is impaled by the boat and sinks to its death, Ellen, now free of the burden, slips beneath the surface but is saved by Hoagie who convinces her not to check out. As Ellen, Hoagie and Michael attempt to stay afloat on the remains of Neptune's Folly, we hear a rescue plane in the distance on its way.

As Ellen boards the plane back to Amity, there is more dialogue between her and Michael about working through their grief about Sean's death plus more random anecdotes from Hoagie who is waiting to take off.

Despite the film's misgivings, it feels like the finished film overall has trimmed the dialogue to greater effect, making some scenes punchier and not messing around with needless exposition. The only major what if, being Hooper's phone call to Michael on Christmas Day.

The Characters

Here we will look at the journey of the main characters throughout Jaws: The Revenge and discuss any interesting plot motifs.

Lynn Whitfield as Louisa and on-screen lover Jake (Mario Van Peebles)

Louisa (Lynn Whitfield) – Louisa, is the wife of Jake, and while largely a peripheral character, she is part of a number of key scenes during *Revenge*.

After Ellen arrives in the Bahamas she is part of a Christmas Day gathering at Michael and Carla's house, with both Jake and Louisa in attendance. From what we can surmise they are both natives of the region and haven't got any children.

Louisa works at the local casino, where Michael and Carla spend New Year's Eve alongside Ellen and Hoagie, who start to show signs of a budding romance.

Louisa's final major scene of the film is during the beach presentation for Carla's sculpture where Thea's banana boat is attacked by the shark. As a supportive friend of the Brody's, she is truly horrified at the attack, with the camera zooming in on her reaction once the shark heads toward the banana boat.

Depending on which ending you believe is the true ending to *Revenge,* we also don't know if she is left a widow, with Jake killed by the shark in one ending and miraculously surviving in another.

Sean Brody (Mitchell Anderson) – Despite having the second name Brody, we sadly don't spend much time with the youngest sibling of Ellen and Martin as he is the first victim of this new deadly shark.

We open the film with Sean and Ellen preparing a fish for dinner, not knowing that the role would soon be reversed. Sean has a brief but warm conversation with Michael and Thea before heading to the Amity Police Department. After thinking he is done for the night, he is asked by receptionist Polly to check out a barge that is caught in the harbour.

Whether you think this is a ruse by the shark is open to debate, but once out on his boat he is quickly attacked and has his left arm torn off in possibly one of the most vicious attacks of the franchise. From here he is quickly dispatched, with his guttural screams drowned out by Christmas carolers.

Despite his short screen time, we can gather that Sean is a warm and caring uncle to Thea, who perhaps doesn't visit as much as he should. He also has the Brody gene of wanting to be in charge, as the Deputy Sheriff of the town, following in his father's footsteps. The most tragic element of Sean's story is the fact that he and his fiance Tiffany (Mary Smith) were planning their wedding before fate intervened. Further adding to the trauma, we hear that Tiffany needed to be sedated after the identification of his body.

Thea Brody (Judith Barsi) – During the late 1980s and early 90s, there was an emerging trope of child characters who were probably too smart for their own good. Thea Brody very much falls into this category. Right from her initial conversation with Ellen and Sean in the opening scenes, it is clear that she has a lot to say for herself, which sometimes could get her in trouble.

We can assume she is roughly around actress Judith Barsi's actual age, 9 years old, and being an only child, is used to getting her own way, which is shown on her return to the Bahamas where she immediately wants to play on the docks with the local kids before being ushered back in by a combination of Ellen and Carla; much to her annoyance.

Given her young age, she clearly does not understand the grieving process, which is most notably displayed when she quizzes Ellen about the now deceased Sean being bad and needing a spanking. While Ellen tries to brush this off (unconvincingly), this instantly creates an atmosphere on Christmas Day, of all days.

With *Revenge* pitched as a direct sequel to the original Jaws, it made total sense for her to have a scene with her father where they imitate each other's actions at the dinner table. Ellen sees this and gets slightly teary.

Thea is part of possibly the most iconic scene of the film as her banana boat is attacked by the shark, but she is saved after Mrs. Ferguson throws herself into danger's way to protect the children.

While Thea appears very close with her grandmother she doesn't mention her late grandfather once, but we feel this is more to put the emphasis of the film on Ellen rather than the departed Martin Brody.

On first watch, you may find the character of Thea quite annoying, but on multiple rewatches, she does form a vital part of the plot and her attack on the banana boat is the straw that breaks the camel's back, which sees Ellen go after the shark on Neptune's Folly.

Michael Caine as Hoagie

Hoagie (Michael Caine) – For those that have read the novelisation of *Revenge,* you will know that Hoagie had an even bigger role to play in the story. Author Hank Searls portrayed the rogue pilot as a secret government agent who transports laundered money while fronting as a pilot.

His role in the film is much linear as he flies the Brody's from Amity to the Bahamas and quickly establishes a connection with Ellen. After a spot of fishing later he paddles ashore in his rowboat and starts to break down Ellen's emotional barriers that she has put up since Sean's death.

Hoagie is very much a free-spirit, full of stories and his positive attitude tries to help Ellen through the grieving process whilst also secretly wanting to establish a romantic relationship with her. His timing is questionable at best, given that she has recently buried her youngest son and remains obsessed with the idea that sharks are hunting her family.

His role in the finale feels largely for comedic effect as he crash-lands his plane in the ocean, before being attacked by the shark;

which promptly sinks it. After surviving the attack he barks orders to Michael, Jake and Ellen, with no one really listening to him as the shark approaches, before being impaled by the bowsprit on the front of the boat.

It is unclear in the final reel as Ellen boards Hoagie's plane whether their budding romance will continue or if it was simply a minor attraction or part of the grieving process for granny Brody.

In production notes for *Revenge*, Caine talked about the middle-age relationship between Ellen and Hoagie, saying,

"It's quite extraordinary, really. I think it's a first for me, being involved with someone my own age in a movie. We have a little flirtatious sort of romance…and the way it turns out, the romance between two-middle-aged people is more like the romance between two teenagers. Being middle-aged, they're probably used to being with one person for so long that they're a bit awkward at dating. So it's rather charming and rather funny."

Carla Brody (Karen Young) – Our initial impressions of Carla are very much rooted in her devotion to Michael whilst also trying to keep Ellen close in the wake of Sean's death. Between Carla and Thea they help to convince her to come to the Bahamas for Christmas.

It would be so easy to paint Carla as a basic housewife, but giving her the job as a potentially award-winning sculptor gives her agency and gives her a level of independence that we didn't see from Ellen in the original Jaws.

Albeit the 'angry welder' that Michael wants to make love to, she also knows how to have a good time and we can surmise that they frequently double date with Jake and Louisa.

Her big moment is certainly trumped by a certain shark, as Carla's sculpture is unveiled on the beach at the same time that Thea is attacked. Carla quickly descends into a frantic, yet helpless parent as she screams for the banana boat to return her daughter to shore. Following the attack she finds out that Michael and Jake knew about the shark and had been tracking it which causes her to lose it and scream at Michael as he leaves to go after his mother, who has stolen Neptune's Folly. We can only imagine what her thoughts were after Michael, Ellen and Hoagie finally reached the shore after killing the shark.

In production notes for *Revenge,* Young talked briefly about the support she had from Joseph Sargent but is less complimentary about the weather conditions in Nassau.

"Not once…have I felt the 'effects' aspects overshadowing the personal elements of the story. And all of the credit for that goes to Joe Sargent. He is simply the best. He really cares about the 'people' part of this film. His biggest concern seems to be making you care about the characters.

"Terrible (weather) but the picture got done. That's what counts. Isn't it?"

Jake (Mario Van Peebles) – While not a Brody, Jake becomes an integral part of the story from his first scene where he both berates Michael for attending his brother's funeral but also says how much he missed him. Jake is seen in one instance as comic relief, but also snappy making him quite schizophrenic, with the viewer unclear which Jake they are getting from scene to scene.

As already stated, it is clear that the Brody's and Jake and Louisa are close, with Jake getting a grant to study sea snails before Michael joined as his marine biologist partner. While pitched as an ambitious scientist, he sees dollar signs when he sees the shark for the first time and comes up with a plan to track it and gain further funding and study something a bit more exciting.

Without hesitation, he joins Michael's crazy quest to find his mother in a tiny rowboat before Hoagie suggests a slightly more conventional option in the form of his plane.

Strangely it is Jake's tracking system which causes the shark's downfall, but not before he is grabbed off the front of the boat and also falls into its gaping jaws. The shark swallows the shock device before grabbing Jake and pulling him under. As we know there were two endings shot for the film, with the alternate showing Jake miraculously escaping from the shark despite being shown being dragged under in its mouth and not being seen again whilst the fish is being shocked to death.

In the wake of this, maybe Jake and Louisa decided to move away and start a new life far away from the ocean?

In production notes for Revenge, Van Peebles speaks of his admiration for his father (who has a minor cameo in the film) and describes Jake as a 'catalyst' and a 'guy who makes things happen, a motivator'.

Michael Brody (Lance Guest) – As our co-lead, Michael Brody is another character who feels tonally all over the place. After arriving in Amity for his brother's funeral, he shows little emotion about his passing and only becomes animated once the idea of Ellen coming to the Bahamas becomes a possibility.

Do we assume that Michael didn't look for the approval of his parents and went out to follow his own path whereas Sean was the hometown boy and stayed to follow in his father's footsteps?

Another strange choice is Michael not having any scar tissue from his harrowing encounter in the estuary with the original shark all those years ago. While it fits the plot narratively, it makes little logical sense for him to have become a marine biologist.

Once we get to the Bahamas we see Michael and Jake's relationship as loving but also with a degree of one-upmanship, with Jake paranoid about being seen as the leader of the program by assistants Clarence and William.

Michael clearly knows the reputation of Hoagie and becomes quite paranoid as they start to spend time alone together. This is almost a role reversal with a son not thinking someone is good enough for his mother whereas stereotypically this would be the mother's role to disapprove of anyone wanting to have a relationship with her son.

His relationship with his daughter Thea, feels distant, with Carla seen as the enforcer or 'bad cop' of the parents. Michael only reinforces her views and can be present late at night to put his daughter to bed, thus fulfilling minor parenting duties.

Much like Ellen, he begins to have nightmares after his first encounter with the Great White but he shows stubbornness or a degree of bravery by getting back into the water the next day to continue the sea snails study. Is this another example of Michael being stubborn and desperately trying to carve his own path without listening to the (logical) requests of others?

While his stubbornness could be seen as a strength, keeping the shark a secret from his family almost proves deadly following the banana boat attack. He apologises profusely to his daughter without giving his wife a full explanation for his actions. Carla loses it with him, and you get the feeling that the aftermath of the finale would have led to some interesting conversations between the pair despite appearing to reconcile as Ellen leaves for Amity.

Michael attempts to get a straight answer out of Ellen after getting to the boat from Hoagie's emergency landing in his plane. You could argue that it is the combination of the Brody's that is the downfall of the Great White, as Michael shocks the shark to the surface before Ellen impales it with part of the ship.

Speaking in the production notes for *Revenge*, Lance Guest describes Michael as 'reckless', saying,

"Michael is a very reckless guy most of the time, but he's very protective of his family. He doesn't want to let his mother know he's seen this thing because he knows how traumatic it would be for her. Yet he can't suppress his own fascination with it. He's a scientist after all and there's never been a Great White spotted in the Bahamas. It's an opportunity of a lifetime for him."

Ellen Brody (Lorraine Gary) – The character of Ellen Brody is taken on an emotional rollercoaster during the duration of *Revenge*. After appearing as a content widow, she is grief-stricken by the surprise death of her youngest son Sean. Without missing a beat she demands that Michael give up his job as a marine biologist and get out of the water. Her irrational theory is that the fear of sharks killed her late husband (who died previously of a heart attack) and a vengeful shark came for Sean.

At Sean's funeral she recalls moments from his childhood trying to remember the good times, whereas his fiance Tiffany is clearly distraught. After she is talked into going to the Bahamas for Christmas, her walls come tumbling down as she crosses the water on the way to the airport. In the early stages of the film it has to be said that Ellen is an accurate portrayal of the tonal imbalance that grief places on a person before she descends into more bizarre behaviour.

Probably the second-best sequence in the film is the scene where Ellen is swimming off the coast and is attacked by the shark. Director Sargent builds adequate suspense coupled with Michael Small's score but this is undercut by us discovering this is just a nightmare. It would certainly have been a bold choice to kill off two Brody's in the film, although it may have made for a more interesting feature with Michael and Jake hunting the shark a la Quint, Hooper and Brody.

She constantly feels on edge and begins to sense the shark's presence, from the point when Michael and Jake's barge is first attacked.

Ellen's relationship with Hoagie begins rather innocently, and even at the film's conclusion, as we have already stated, we aren't sure how serious either party was taking it.

The two spend some time together at a Bahamas street festival where Ellen is given a pep talk by Hoagie to 'give it a kick in the arse' and get on with her life, but this is quickly undercut by her bizarre connection to the shark.

She does show signs of recovery as she and Michael reconcile at the casino on New Year's Eve and at the close of the night, she also kisses Hoagie goodnight, potentially setting up a new romance.

The strange thing about her connection to the shark, is that she does not detect its presence at the beach until its dorsal fin surfaces and starts to head for Thea on the banana boat. Ellen is the one to alert everyone at the beach as she screams for her granddaughter. As we know this is the moment she finally takes charge of her destiny and starts on her irrational journey to kill the shark.

Stealing Michael's boat she ventures to sea where she goads the shark and still appears shocked when it attacks the boat.

Once Michael, Jake and Hoagie arrive she finally has shipmates with a remote sense of what to do, and despite Jake's apparent death she unbeknownst combines with Michael to shock and impale the shark on the boat. Depending on what ending you see, she also inexplicably caused the shark to explode too.

With her trauma buried at the bottom of the Bahamas ocean, she can now return to Amity, asking her family to return for a holiday this summer. The question is, once she arrives back on the island will her grief over Sean's death take hold, also will she be there for Sean's widow Tiffany who has seemingly been forgotten about since the funeral?

Gary spoke about returning to the role of Ellen in the production notes for *Revenge*, saying,

"There are real people in this movie who care very much about each other. It's an action movie, of course, but it's also about relationships which I think makes it much more like the first 'Jaws.'"

Speaking of her on-screen romance with Caine, Gary commented, "The first day we were to work together I was nervous as a schoolgirl. We were shooting a Junkanoo Festival with noisy drums and hundreds of extras. But he never faltered in his concentration and he put me completely at ease. It was all so natural. He's an extraordinary actor – and just a nice human being."

Michael Caine and the Oscar Debacle

Michael Caine filming the finale of Jaws: The Revenge, instead of receiving an oscar

The original plan was for filming to be complete on Jaws 4 by the end of March 1987, allowing Michael Caine to attend the Academy Awards ceremony on 30th March and receive his Best Supporting Actor accolade for his role in Hannah and Her Sisters.

These plans were swiftly halted when weather problems in Nassau slowed the production of Jaws down, causing Caine to miss the show.

Marilyn Beck reported in the Democrat and Chronicle (9th April edition) that Michael Caine would also be set to miss the start of rehearsals for Switching Channels, an American comedy starring Christopher Reeve, because he didn't know when filming would be complete on Jaws: The Revenge.

A source at Universal told Beck,

"We're on alert. If the weather settles down next week or the week after, we expect to return to the Bahamas with a skeleton first unit crew and most of the principles. Caine's scenes should definitely be done there instead of a studio backlot or sound stage."

Ultimately, Caine missed the awards ceremony at the Dorothy Chandler Pavilion in Los Angeles and co-host Sigourney Weaver accepted the award on his behalf.

Nate Jones interviewed Caine for an article on 26th October 2010 for Time.com, where the actor addressed the Oscar debacle saying,

"Hannah and her Sisters came out in the dumping period of January and February. It did well, it got very good reviews, but there was no [Oscar] campaign. I'd taken a part that was a week in a movie, which I'd done several times before. They (Universal) said, 'We're making this film about Jaws, will you do seven days on that?' [The Oscars] came out of the blue; I was astonished that I was nominated. I went to Universal and said, 'Can you change the schedule?' and they said no: 'We can't, because we're stuck with the boats and the traps.' And so I had to be there, and so I missed it."

In production notes for *Revenge*, Caine made light of missing the ceremony but says it was simply part of being in the film industry. He did, however, find minor consolation in the fact he was filming in the Bahamas.

While promoting his role in the TV mini-series adaptation of 20000 Leagues Under the Sea in 1997, Caine reflected on his role with Starlog magazine.

"I came in and played a little part for two weeks. The series had been pretty good and done pretty well. Someone asked me if I wanted to go to the Bahamas and do a guest shot in the film, so I did it," he said.

"What frustrates me is that people made it sound like I made this great career choice to play this gigantic lead part in Jaws 4. I've never seen the movie. I really don't know what the rest of the movie is about. I just went to the Bahamas and did my little guest shot."

Spielberg Gives His Blessing

Although unclear in the timeline, Steven Spielberg would take a look at the script for Jaws: The Revenge and according to Sargent, sent him the following note,

"Like the Vietnam vet, I came home too and managed never to think about the year 1974, until I started reading 'Jaws: The Revenge.' Got to Page 18 and found myself holding that service revolver and discharging it until empty into the Atlantic Ocean. I just couldn't go on reading because it brought back so many memories.

"Good luck, Joseph Sargent. Bring a lot of Joseph Conrad to read while you're waiting for the next shoot.

"Call home often to talk to people you love.

"With tremendous sympathy and two winks of my right eye, (signed) Steve."

The Press Circuit Starts

Publicity for Jaws '87 began slightly before cameras started rolling in Edgartown.

Mario Van Peebles was featured on MTV in January 1987 in what is probably the first television advertisement for the film. Speaking about the 'Jaws 87' project and playing Jake, he said,

"They wanted actors that didn't have good taste but did taste good. I play a Bahamian marine biologist, which is fun because I lived in Negril for quite some time so I got the accent, so it's no problem. (This is) sort of the brown answer to the Richard Dreyfuss role in the first film, and they got me with the dreadlocks and glasses and everything so it's another character role for me.

The Charlotte Observer ran a feature by Anne Thompson on 13th May discussing the contenders for the summer blockbuster dollars; including Jaws: The Revenge.

"Another strong summer entry is Universal's sequel to the Spielberg classic, 'Jaws: The Revenge,' minus Roy Scheider. Lorraine Gary will return with the film, and Michael Caine will make his 'Jaws' debut as Gary's love interest," Thompson commented.

Louisville, Kentucky's The Courier Journal announced on 5th July that Darryl's 1815 Restaurant and Bar 3110 Bardstown Road would be holding a special promotional event for Jaws: The Revenge until 15th July. Staff from the restaurant would hand out posters and other paraphernalia plus two passes for the 16th July premiere.

This grand prize would also consist of limo service from the winner's home to the local Showcase Cinemas, a free dinner at Darryl's plus a return trip in the limo home. To be eligible, entrants needed to be 13 years or older and fill out a questionnaire about the Jaws franchise which would be handed out by Darryl's staff.

From the 5th July Universal Pictures ran competitions in newspapers across America, including the St Louis Post Dispatch with readers encouraged to register in the Young Men's Department of any Famous-Barr store between 7th and 14h July for the chance to win one of five pairs of tickets to the film's premiere.

Mario Van Peebles briefly appeared in a column of the 24th May edition of The Morning News Sun, discussing his water scenes in Jaws: The Revenge,

"I'll go in the water with my clothes on. I've done that many times, as long as you don't have anything else to do the rest of the day."

Van Peebles was also interviewed about his role in *Revenge* in the 16th July 1987 edition of The Daily News, saying,

"The acting in the second and third 'Jaws' films was so bad that I found myself talking to the screen, saying to the shark 'Eat them, please'. But the producers had seen my work in Clint Eastwood's 'Heartbreak Ridge' and they knew I'd create a lot of it myself, so they offered me double the money I usually get and let me create my own character.

He continued,

"It's totally different than my roles in other films and on 'LA Law'. People don't realize I'm the same guy."

Plans were coming together for the premiere of Jaws: The Revenge, with Dorsey Griffith reporting for California's The Modesto Bee that local Martha's Vineyard school Nathan Mayhew Seminars had secured the first local screening on 16th July at the Island Theatre in Oak Bluffs, operated by Lockwood Theatres Inc.

Bidding for this illustrious right was big news across the Vineyard with several institutions vying for the screening, including Vineyard Environmental Research Institute and Martha's Vineyard Historical Preservation Society. It was revealed that Norma Bridwell, Chairman of the Seminars fundraising committee had spoken to Roger Lockwood, who owned Lockwood Theatres Inc, which operated the Island Theatre in March about the potential screening.

Lockwood then contacted Universal Pictures and managed to secure the premiere before any of the other interested parties submitted a formal bid.

Tickets for the premiere at the Island Theatre cost $25 each, with a champagne reception following at the Atlantic Connection.

Joseph Sargent spoke of the appeal of the Jaws franchise in the documentary, Behind the Scenes of Jaws the Revenge, a WSBK-TV production directed by William Rus, which screened on 10th July 1987.

"I think the appeal of the Jaws films is primarily about the intense identification with that primal terror that's in all of us. Being eaten alive in the middle of the ocean and we somehow can't swim fast enough away."

Van Peebles continued to be a large part of the promotion for Jaws: The Revenge, as he was the cover star of the 27th July 1987 edition of Jet magazine, which featured news, culture and entertainment features focusing on the African-American community.

The actor's starring role in the fourth film in the Jaws franchise was billed as him breaking into the big time, as part of a major studio production.

He discussed the casting of his father Melvin, who has a cameo in Revenge as Mr Witherspoon in the Bahamas town where Jake resides.

"For years I've been hearing, 'Well, the only reason you got anywhere is you're Melvin's son.' So now it's funny to get my old man in," Van Peebles said.

Ebony magazine also featured Van Peebles in the November 1987 edition discussing coming out from under his father's shadow with his role in Jaws: The Revenge plus his recurring role in television series LA Law.

Despite a scathing review in the March 1988 edition of Cinefantastique Magazine, Steve Biodrowski ran a two-page feature discussing the special effects used in the film; entitled The Tale of Two Sharks for Jaws: The Revenge.

Biodrowski takes an interesting stance on the film, which at this point had already been savaged by critics, focusing on the conflict between director Sargent and Ted Rae and Tim Lawrence, who were hired to create miniatures.

Rae said Sargent told him,

"We can't use that it looks like we shot a real shark against a blue screen and matted it into the shot."

While Rae argued about the care that was taken in creating the shark, Sargent argued that the shark didn't resemble the full-scale models created for the action sequences.

With Jaws: The Revenge getting plenty of publicity pre-release, it was now time to chum the waters for the critics…

Reviews and Critical Response

Michael and Jake await the reviews of Jaws: The Revenge...

It may be easy to assume that the critical response to Jaws: The Revenge was wholly negative but there were some journalists who looked favorably on it when it hit screens on 17th July 1987.

Terry Lawson of the Dayton Daily News said,

"Jaws The Revenge is a bloody cut above the usual. Because anyone buying a ticket knows what he's in for, we have to give the filmmakers niggling credit for delivering the goods."

Lawson also heaped praise on director Joseph Sargent, who he described as having a 'decent sense of timing and commercial bent.'

Barbara Vancheri wrote in the Pittsburgh Post Gazette that Revenge lacked the star power of Scheider to drive a fairly ludicrous story forward.

"Jaws the Revenge lacks a figure like Scheider to carry the plot. Caine's character is minor and while (Lance) Guest is good, he can't ignite a story that doesn't exist. Even the backdrop of the Bahamas and fascinating underwater sequences don't help.

"After Jaws 1,2, 3D and now 4 let the creature rest in peace – and pieces," Vancheri noted.

The Fort Worth Star Telegram gave the film a favorable 6 out of 10, but said 'can range from thrilling to numbing in terms of entertainment value.'

Linnea Lannon didn't hold back in her review of the film in the 19th July edition of the Detroit Free Press, leading with the headline 'Boredom is the biggest threat in Jaws the Revenge'.

"The great failing of Jaws the Revenge? You don't scream and you don't laugh. This 'Jaws' isn't scary enough to be taken seriously and isn't camp enough to be funny. Even if you are rooting for the shark," Lannon noted.

The 20th July edition of the Philadelphia Daily News was also not impressed, saying this could help prevent future Jaws sequels, little did they know...

"In a way, it's a good thing that this sequel is as dumb, dull and just plain bad as it is. It's bound to be a box-office dud, and maybe that'll spare us 'Jaws V'. No stars."

Notorious film critic Roger Ebert reviewed the film for the Lexington Herald Leader and was scathing of both the acting and the design of the shark.

"Since we see so much of the shark in the movie, you'd think they would have built some good ones. They've had three earlier pictures for practice. But in some scenes, the shark's skin looks like (a) canvas with acne, and in others, all we see is an obviously fake shark head with lots of teeth," he said.

Steve Dollar of the Green Bay Gazette described the film as 'listless as a rudderless boat at low tide'.

He also was not a fan of Gary's return to the big screen, saying she was not a character you feel compelled to watch.

Mark Cartwright, writing for the 23rd July edition of the Jordan Valley Sentinel praised the film, saying,

"Jaws the Revenge still manages to make you jump in your seat and, of course, scream in the right places. The cast including Michael Caine is good and the shark isn't anyone to take lightly."

Joe Bob Briggs took a more humorous approach to his review of the film, in the El Paso Times on 24th July.

"The only problem with this movie is the shark never eats Lorraine (Gary). In fact, the shark seems like he's on a diet or something. He doesn't eat much of the cast at all, even though he had a golden opportunity to eat the obnoxious little girl."

On the same day, the Pensacola News Journal took aim at Michael Caine's role in the film, saying he will basically accept anything he is offered at this stage.

"What's Michael Caine doing here, you may well ask. Wasting his time, of course. He's a beach-combing pilot, and this is one of those roles he takes just because he seems to have made a resolution to take anything offered," the review said.

Despite a number of scathing reviews, Lorraine Gary hit back at critics of Jaws: The Revenge in the 25th July edition of The News Pilot, telling Marilyn Beck,

"The thought of a husband making a $30 million movie as a present to a middle-aged wife is ridiculous. My husband is too good a businessman for that. If he were going to do something like that, why not do that 15 years ago when I still had a face and a body.

"Last year the 'Jaws' role just dropped into my lap. Sid came home one night and said he was going to make 'Jaws IV' and did I want to be in it?'

Beck also notes in this article that Gary was looking to continue her career in Hollywood but in a producer role rather than in front of the camera.

"I'm not in the business of looking for work. Those days are gone," Gary concluded.

Christopher Martin reviewed the film for the March 1988 edition of Cinemafantastique, saying,

"This movie shows Steven Spielberg at his very best...simply because he had nothing to do with it.

"As promised in the promos, this sequel is about people...and those people do some remarkably stupid things for the sake of the plot."

With critics largely taking chunks out of Jaws: The Revenge, the question now was how would it perform with audiences?

Jaws fan Shaun O'Rourke with one of the models used in Jaws: The Revenge

Despite the critical panning of the film, one of the full-scale shark models used in the film was put out for display at the Government Center in Boston, Massachusetts in September 1987 before being moved to the city's Museum of Science to help promote the opening of the special effects exhibit, starting on 5th October at the City Hall Plaza. The flyer for the exhibit would feature 'Bruce' on its cover, with the event also showcasing props from films such as Aliens, King Kong and Ghostbusters.

In the 26th December edition of Billboard Magazine, Jaws: The Revenge's home video release was announced with a full page spread promoting the VHS and Laserdisc release, scheduled for 4th February 1988.

MCA Home Video released Jaws: The Revenge on VHS in the US, as previously mentioned in February '88, with the interesting addition of brand new footage not seen in the cinematic release. The VHS version of the film (and subsequent DVD and Blu Ray) con-

Release

Jake is ready to feed the shark
(and audiences) a meal they won't forget

Jaws: The Revenge was released in 1606 cinemas across America on 17th July 1987, with an opening weekend gross of $7.1 million, debuting at third place in the US Box Office. It slumped to sixth spot the following week before closing its theatrical run in 12th spot.

The final domestic gross was $20.7 million, from a budget of $23 million. Revenge did fairly well overseas with an international gross of $31.1 million meaning that the film had an overall gross of $51.8 million, which taking into account inflation equates to a healthy $107.5 million gross.

tained just over a minute of new footage plus a new ending where the shark inexplicably explodes after being hit with Neptune's Folly, being steered by Ellen Brody.

MCA would run promotional adverts on US network television at this time, proclaiming, 'the terror is back, the fear is real, the screams more chilling and the attack more deadly' and that it was 'the most frightening Jaws of all.'

CIC Video, who had previously handled releases of the three previous Jaws films plus multiple parts of the Friday the 13th series, released Jaws: The Revenge on home video in the UK.

Revenge was reviewed in Video Review Magazine in March 1988, an issue which included the film's #9 debut on the VHS charts plus a full-page spread advertising the film's physical media release on VHS and laserdisc.

Reviewer Jeffrey Lyons was less than complimentary, giving the film one-star in a scathing review, saying,

"Jaws: The Revenge is about as inane as it gets. Seeing it again on videotape, with inconsequential new scenes added since its theatrical release, I kept wishing they'd just leave the first one alone and swim away.

"Jaws: The Revenge takes its revenge, all right – on all who see it."

William Guidry reviewed the VHS of *Revenge* for the March 1988 edition of Conservative Digest, saying,

"Jaws: The Revenge victimises the audience as well as what little remains of the human leftovers from previous assaults."

Video Today Magazine featured *Revenge* as their cover feature in the April 1988 edition, with CIC Video running a competition to win one of 10 copies on VHS.

In a double-page feature, Chris Adam-Smith had this to say about the film,

"It is hard to believe that so many seemingly bright people can get themselves into such a bouillabaisse over a fish. Still, I suppose when that fish happens to be a 25ft great white shark with a set of teeth to rival Gary Busey's, an appetite like Desperate Dan's and the mangy disposition of Jason Voorhees it is about time to get scared.

"A cheerfully brisk film cut to 90 minutes from 100 for its theatrical release. It should do quite well for CIC on video whatever the running time comes out at."

Video Review Magazine would also run a follow-up article in their May 1988 edition, revealing that the videotape and laserdisc release would feature a brand-new ending, shot exclusively for European cinematic audiences and the home video release.

Speaking about Mario Van Peebles' Jake's apparent resurrection in the finale, the article states,

"But test audiences baulked at seeing Mario turned into shark food, so he was asked to return to the set and reprise his role as a marine biologist. The video version resurrects his character. We wonder if the laser disc version will feature both endings like *Topaz* does."

Film Review 1988-89 featured a short review of the film, stating,

"The finale is uproarious farce, nearly swamping some surprisingly good performances from a cast that includes Michael Caine and Lorraine Gary."

The DVD release of *Revenge* happened on 1st February 2005, featuring the previously used theatrical ending with a blu-ray release on 11th July 2016 with the same 'special feature'.

The August 2016 edition of Home Cinema Choice magazine ran a full-page spread about the simultaneous release of all of the Jaws sequels on Blu Ray. While *Revenge* is mentioned by writer Anton van Beek, the focus of the article is more about Jaws 3D having the option to watch the film in 3D.

In their next issue in September 2016, Home Cinema Choice ran a double-page review of the Jaws sequel trilogy. Speaking about *Revenge*, the reviewer states,

"Sadly as woeful as the movie is, it doesn't deserve to be treated as badly as it is here. While colours are accurate, the 2.40:1 image shows clear signs of digital noise reduction throughout, wiping out grain and fine detail in equal measure.

"Jaws: The Revenge delivers a DTS-HD MA 5.1 mix that lifts the (all-too infrequent) action with effective panning effects and modest LFE support.

"Easily the worst of the lot – both as a movie and Blu-Ray. Digital scrubbing ahoy!"

Rue Morgue also covered the Blu Ray release of the Jaws sequels, with a full-page spread in their September 2016 issue entitled Writer Bites Shark.

John W. Bowen took a more tongue-in-cheek look at the *Revenge*, saying,

"...Jaws: The Revenge is truly a heckler's holiday, which is sort of an endorsement around here. Now smile, you sonofabitch, and get the hell out of my basement."

Finally, in August 2021 UK retailer Zavvi released a steelbook Blu Ray edition of *Revenge*, which simply features the textless poster for the film with Ellen looking to impale the shark but no other unique features were added to this release.

We still await the 4K restoration release…

Taking a Bite out of the Razzies

Bruce Jnr is ready to take a bite out of the 1988 Razzies

Every year The Razzies aka the Golden Raspberry Awards nominates the worst performances and films for its parody of the Academy Awards.

Beginning in 1981, the ceremony was founded by UCLA film graduates and industry veterans John J.B Wilson and Mo Murphy.

Unlike the coveted Academy Awards trophies, the Golden Raspberry Awards featured a golf ball-sized atop a mangled super 8 film reel, which had been spray-painted gold.

Talking to the 18th February 1988 edition of the St. Louis Dispatch, Wilson explained the criteria of being nominated for a Razzie, saying,

"There are three basic theories of what qualifies as a Razzie. First, Hollywood's own measure, how much money did it lose? Second, a movie that was not supposed to be a comedy that generated enormous laughs from the audience. 'Jaws' was one of those and so was Norman Mailer's Tough Guys Don't Dance, which was laughed off the screen in Cannes.

"The last is how excruciating it is to actually sit through a film. Does someone have to pay you money or bribe you with popcorn? 'Who's That Girl?' fits into that category."

The eighth annual Golden Raspberry Awards took place on 29th March 1988, with Jaws: The Revenge holding the joint record with nominations in seven categories. The film did win one of these awards, with Henry Millar 'winning' the Worst Visual Effects gong.

Revenge was also nominated for Worst Picture, losing out to Leonard Part 6 (starring Bill Cosby) and comically for Worst Actor for 'Bruce' the shark, which was also bagged by Cosby. Lorraine Gary was nominated for Worst Actress but lost out to Madonna's turn in Who's That Girl. Michael Caine was nominated for Worst Supporting Actress, with that award being taken home by David Mendenhall in the Stallone vehicle Over The Top. Joseph Sargent was up for Worst Director but this award went jointly to Norman Mailer for Tough Guys Don't Dance and Elaine May for Ishtar. Leonard Part 6 won its third trophy of the night, with Jonathan Reynolds receiving the Worst Screenplay ahead of Michael De Guzman for *Revenge*.

The ceremony for the Golden Raspberry Awards took place on 19th April 1988, with no cast and crew from Jaws: The Revenge attending to receive their awards.

In a strange alternative scenario, Lorraine Gary was also nominated for a Saturn Award, which honoured the best science fiction, fantasy and horror films of the year. The awards ceremony took place on 23rd August 1988, with Jessica Tandy's portrayal of Faye Riley in Batteries Not Included scooping this award ahead of Gary.

Jaws: The Revenge Exhumed

Jaws: The Revenge was supposed to be a back-to-basics sequel...

From the opening in the docks of Amity, it is clear that Joseph Sargent wanted this film to feel like a back to basics sequel. While Michael Small's score soars during the opening credits, it is very strange to see an italic version of the title card which has the feel of a TV movie and not one with $23 million behind it.

We get the impression from the outset that the shark is navigating the bay, perhaps waiting for Sean Brody, although this is a theory I dispute to an extent.

Speaking of Sean, we get our introduction to both the youngest Brody and Ellen and find out within what feels like 10 seconds that she is now a widow by her description of her husband being the biggest tomato thief of all time which is delivered with an odd poignancy. This is very much a woman who has accepted her partner has gone, but at the same time seems to have daily reminders of their life together.

The relationship between Sean and Ellen is extremely warm from the outset, and we get the feeling that they both play up to each other's eccentricities. This is shown when Sean cuts himself whilst chopping vegetables and she instinctively checks if he is okay – a mother's work is never done I guess.

The assumption I made is that Sean is perhaps between moving out or still living at home, while he and his fiance Tiffany plan their future together.

When Ellen picks up the phone and it's her granddaughter Thea, we get an incline of the diversity between the Brody brothers. Here we have Sean, still living in Amity and following in his father's footsteps working for the Police Department whereas Michael has gotten out and is training to become a Marine Biologist. Sean teases him about his work and you get the feeling this is the banter that has been going on for years. Polar opposites in many ways but bonded by blood.

Thea is already, without being physically on-screen, clearly following a popular trope of 1980s children who have a lot to say for themselves despite their young age. To make a connection back to the original Jaws director – this character almost feels plucked straight out of E.T.

The timeline is slightly unclear here as Ellen, Sean and Tiffany walk through the village but again this feels like Sargent laying the groundwork of the Brody's being the heartbeat once again of the series. Interestingly, Sean debates with Ellen about their Christmas tree and seasonal traditions, with Sean very much into the idea of a traditional festive period. This feels like another example of them playing off against each other, which is made more believable by the on-screen chemistry of Lorraine Gary and Mitchell Anderson.

Sean checks in at the Police Station and we meet Polly (recast as Edna Billotto), who sends him out to check on a piece of wood that has become stuck on the channel marker just off the docks. We do get a passing mention of Lenny, who we assume is the same character from the first two films (played by Jeffrey Kramer) who can't deal with the issue because he is cow tipping at Ben Masters' place.

As Sean arrives at the docks, he walks through the choir (singing pretty badly according to the choirmaster) and mentions briefly about his time as a shepherd, which harks back to this idea he is a one-town man and working in the Police force means he is a pillar, of sorts of the community.

I don't read into the theory that the shark somehow placed the plank of wood on the channel marker mainly because it is physically impossible (but so is a roaring shark I hear you say), plus it's much scarier that this was sheer coincidence.

The attack itself is arguably the most visceral and violent of the series, with Sargent employing rapid cuts which although quite jarring would mimic an attack far better than the slow-motion employed later on. Sean's initial delayed reaction to losing his arm is also horrifying, with the camera almost waiting for him to notice before zooming in on the damage. As Sean screams for help his cries are drowned out by the choir on the shore, which could be read as a metaphor for Christmas itself blocking out negative energies such as another potential shark crisis in Amity.

Given the warmth of the earlier scenes between Ellen and Sean, her identification of his remains (which we only allude to under a sheet) is probably equally as horrifying as the attack. Ellen looks utterly distraught and lost, which is only intensified by Polly crying as she takes off from the police station.

In the original film, we see Hooper look at the remains of Chrissie and even sees her arm, but here Sargent shows some restraint and knows that what the audience imagines is far scarier than what he could reveal under the sheet.

The Story of Jaws: The Revenge • 91

Once Michael, Carla and Thea arrive in Amity for Sean's funeral the dynamic shifts for Ellen who on first seeing her eldest son again, clings onto him for dear life. In many ways (despite the departure later on) Ellen's portrayal of a grieving mother is fairly accurate. Despite being older, it is still an impossible scenario that no parent wants to deal with.

As Michael goes to talk to Ellen who has been standing outside for hours according to Mrs Kittner (the returning Leo Fierro), Thea tries to offset the somber mood. While adults deal with grieving in different ways, children (especially 5-year-olds) can't really understand loss yet, which is evident by her asking if Sean will ever come back – a naive yet heartbreaking comment.

What is interesting is that Carla feels quite restrained as she leaves Michael to comfort Ellen, which can be read as either a distant relationship or simply not getting involved in a close and sensitive family matter.

Ellen's mindset, which to be fair can be read as the state of shock, seems to flip once Michael arrives, as she talks of the shark coming for Sean. The statement makes very little sense and is quickly dispelled by Michael later on.

Later on, she again tries to put a brave face on and thrust herself into cooking a fettuccine dish for the family, with Carla trying to convince her to relax. She gets herself into a rut and demands that Michael gives up his marine biologist job whilst claiming again Sean was chosen by the shark plus Martin Brody, who Michael reveals died from a heart attack. Ellen's fairly baseless claims can still be read as part of the grieving process which kind of gets out of hand later on.

In the lead-up to Sean's funeral, Michael and Carla walk along the beach near the Brody house and start to talk about the Brody boys' childhood before Michael randomly starts to run down the beach. Is this Michael's stress release? The scene itself feels a bit abrupt and one wonders if there was more to this scene that ended up on the cutting room floor.

Sean's funeral is a somber affair with two almost polar opposites of grief, as we have Tiffany (who we found out earlier needed to be sedated after the news of his death) who is crying her eyes out whereas Ellen is trying to remember good times from Sean's childhood and again put on a brave face for her family and the people of Amity who have turned out in force.

In an attempt to take Ellen's mind off Sean, Michael suggests she comes back to the Bahamas with them and after being asked by both Thea and Carla she abruptly agrees, perhaps without fully thinking it through. Presumably, Tiffany is left to grieve with her own family as she is never seen or mentioned again after the funeral.

While using the car to travel to the mainland, Thea asks Ellen to swing her around which quickly turns into a family affair as Carla then Michael joins in. For a split second, Ellen is happy and smiling but once her family turns away she seems to recoil into a grief-stricken state, clearly feeling guilty for being momentarily happy at such a time.

On the way to Nassau, Ellen can be seen staring blankly out of the window which is clearly making the rest of the Brody's uncomfortable. You get the feeling she maybe has not said anything for a prolonged period of time and is wearing big dark shades. This is very much Ellen covering up, with the theory that the eyes are the windows to the soul and if blocked she can maintain a barrier to anyone who wants to break down the walls.

We are introduced to Hoagie as he is harassed by Thea, who like any five year old has become bored and started to ask lots of questions – including if she can fly the plane. Michael gives us some exposition on Hoagie as a carefree gambler, which is quickly brushed off as he will 'get it back next time'.

Hoagie breaks the ice with Ellen before taking them for a quick up and down ride before landing. This off-beat character is clearly jarring to Ellen and as we know later on becomes a potential romantic interest, perhaps due to his relaxed demeanor.

Once the family arrive back, Thea charges off to the dock to play with the neighbours on the rope swing. As soon as Ellen lays eyes on her swinging towards the sea she can only think 'shark bait' and asks her to come down. Carla sees this and asks nicely and Thea throws a real tantrum, perhaps showing that she is used to getting her own way as she is dragged inside kicking and screaming.

Michael attempts to placate Ellen, who is now blaming herself for causing a rift between Carla and her daughter, by showing her Carla's sculpture which from some angles could resemble a shark's form. This is not really the best way to get her back on-side.

One of the finest sequences in the film is Ellen's nightmare sequence as she is swimming off-shore in Nassau and suddenly becomes paranoid she is being stalked. What Sargent does really well here is mixing POV shots from the shark's perspective with shots from eye level on top of the water where you won't see anything coming from below until it is too late. Much like the Sean attack at the start of the film, this is quick and visceral.

We are introduced to Jake, Michael's research partner as Michael looks for conch off the coast on their barge. Michael is using the yellow submersible, which will continue to play a role later on. Jake comes across as a very driven yet conflicted individual whereas Michael is more relaxed yet meticulous. Their clash, once Michael comes back aboard, is quite bizarre as Jake seemingly blames Michael for leaving him alone to do their work whilst attending his younger brother's funeral. Even more bizarre is their fast reconciliation which is almost child-like, where one minute they are at each other's throats and next they are best of friends.

It is now Christmas day at the Brody house with Ellen regaling the group with embarrassing stories from Michael's childhood. Her popular stories are quickly stunted by Thea asking if Uncle Sean was ever bad and needed spanking? This causes Ellen to almost freeze in fear and then leave the room, with her granddaughter tearing down one of the walls she had put up to forget about her son's death.

During this scene, we also meet Louisa, Jake's partner as the couples quite openly discuss their sex lives, which again feels a tad awkward with both Ellen and Thea in the room.

Michael goes out to talk Ellen round and they have their last proper conversation about Sean as Michael mentions how much he misses him. Ellen once again pleads with him to change professions insisting he is all she has left, which strikes quite a tone. Here is a mother and a grandmother literally clinging onto her last strand of her family whilst negotiating this crazy theory about a series of sharks hunting her family – such a dichotomy. Interestingly, their conversation about Sean is overlaid with Louisa leading the family with 'Hark the Herald Angels Sing' carol which feels quite ironic as Sean's screams for help were drowned out by Christmas carols back in Amity.

Following their conversation, almost doubling down on Ellen's concerns, we get our first proper look at the shark as it seems to be on the way to Nassau. The model does look quite menacing and a bit more agile than scenes later on plus we navigate most of its body to give you a hint at the sheer size of the fish.

Soon after Ellen is helping Thea to build sandcastles on the beach and she senses the shark's presence for the first time. She becomes frozen in fear in the water as Hoagie rows ashore and the two start to discuss Ellen's outlandish theory. Hoagie's more understanding nature helps Ellen let her walls down and she suggests a trip out on his plane. Meanwhile, Michael watches from the dock as he and Jake discuss funding options for their future work.

One aspect of Jaws: The Revenge that it can either be lambasted or praised for is its portrayal of a budding romance between aging characters. Given the fact that Sean is dead and it appears that both Michael and Jake's characters are happily married, this is a fascinating choice by writer Michael De Guzman to put focus on Ellen and Hoagie's relationship.

After another flippant decision, we find Ellen and Hoagie aboard his plane and he asks her to take the wheel, which can be read as a metaphor for taking charge of her life and trying to move on rather than be governed by fear. Hoagie, ever the man of taste, takes Ellen to a local street festival known as a Junkanoo. From here we cut back and forth to Jake in the submersible, being teased by Michael in a flip of their previous interaction whilst tagging conch.

Jake is startled by the shark butting the side of the submersible but instead of going for him it breaches and goes for the part of the barge where Michael is, biting large parts out of it. Back at the Junkanoo, Ellen becomes frozen in fear as her last child is threatened by the shark. The shark model once again looks great, with Sargent using quick cuts coupled with a dramatic score touch from Small, creating quite the suspenseful scene. The only strange takeaway is the fact when the shark goes back under the water there is a pool of blood, even though it never attacked anything that bled.

Once her trance-like state has subsided, Ellen once again tries to throw Hoagie off the scent, which he sees through quite easily and tells her to give it a kick in the backside and get on with her life.

Michael is in shock after the encounter with the shark but Jake, ever the opportunist, smells money and an attempt to do something different than tagging the conch all day.

This eventful day ends with Hoagie bringing Ellen home and being the gentleman he is, shaking hands on what could be called their first date. Depending on where you sit about their relationship this can be quite sweet or just a bit cheesy. What neither of them sees is Michael curtain-twitching at the bedroom window, still very wary of Hoagie. Carla has other things on her mind as she entices her husband back to bed by flicking her pants at him. Sex is clearly the perfect distraction.

The story has jumped a few days and it is now New Year's Eve and we see Michael, Carla, Ellen and Jake entering the casino where Louisa works. There is a small commotion across the room and they recognise Hoagie at the roulette tables. Only building on Hoagie's care-free, all or nothing approach he bets everything and loses but again is quite blase about it, inviting himself along to what turns out to be Louisa's birthday party too.

Continuing the theme of sex being the perfect distraction, Louisa gives Jake an indication of what she wants for her birthday.

Jake almost lets the cat out of the bag regarding the shark (despite being told to keep it a secret by Michael earlier) but is warded off by Louisa who has banned work talk. This gives us the indication that because Jake is so passionate about his work, he will often take it home with him, much to his wife's annoyance.

Hoagie invites Ellen to dance, which seems to be instantly undercut by Michael taking Hoagie's place. What could be classed as cock blocking by Michael turns into quite a tender scene as Ellen reconciles with her son, having turned over a new leaf and asking him to show her what a good dancer he is. Whatever you say about Jaws: The Revenge, it does have some tender family scenes.

The end of this scene is quite odd, as it seems like Ellen's paranoia has been transferred into Michael post his encounter with the shark aboard the barge.

Clearly, the best way to get rid of a hangover is working in the sunshine as we see Jake working on a transmitter as Michael gets on board the next day. The duo makes a compromise on a split of studying the conch and the shark, given how rare Great Whites are in the Bahamas.

Michael's apprehension continues as he gets home and is grilled by Carla on taking out the rubbish bags. You have to applaud the man's sheer audacity of claiming his brain is shrinking as the reason he didn't take out the garbage.

Continuing the theme that sex is the best distraction, Michael woos Carla, claiming he always wanted to make love to an angry welder ever since his childhood. Of all the crazy lines and narratives in this script, this has got to be one of the most bizarre. Having said this, it works and they seemingly get down and dirty, in the garage behind Carla's sculpture with the doors wide open.

Now that Jake and Michael have agreed on studying the Great White, the next day William, one of their assistants, is chumming the waters to entice the shark in so Jake can tag it. Sargent again employs the age-old POV shots as the shark approaches the boat but once the crew spots it, it feels like the model is simply floating towards them and looks less and less life-like. Michael once again becomes frozen in fear as the tagged shark starts to swim away, and we start to hear its heartbeat, which is a plot device that becomes important during the finale.

Meanwhile, Hoagie continues to woo Ellen with some day drinking, offering her a trip to the Caribbean for a few days. He offers to take his manager's plane without his permission, again adding to his 'rebel' personality trait and while she is a bit averse to the trip the pair do share their first kiss.

Now the shark can be tracked, Jake attempts to follow it but they lose it after Michael starts asking questions about Hoagie, still paranoid he isn't good enough for his mother. Michael also hints at his shady past and the fact no one knows much about him plus there are plenty of drug dealers in Nassau. This minor plot motif was surely the inspiration for Hank Searls' side plot in the novelisation with Hoagie being an undercover agent to rat out drug dealers in Nassau.

Ellen has arrived home and has (probably her first on-screen) direct discussion with Carla about the kiss from Hoagie. Carla, much like her husband, feels very blase about it and tells her to embrace the moment and not overthink it. We get the sense here that Ellen and Martin were married for a very long time and were potentially high school sweethearts, meaning she probably hadn't dated anyone else for about 30 years or so.

Ellen does make one significant comment, which can be read as meta, saying,

'I feel too old to be in this thing' – which could be read as Gary's apprehension about returning to acting after such a significant break.

Carla breaks up the talk with more discussion about her own sex life, which again feels a bit odd when she's talking to her mother-in-law.

The shark hoodoo is definitely passed on to Michael as he starts having nightmares about the Great White, showing how the fear and paranoia from Ellen are becoming infectious.

Presumably the next night, Michael is working at the dinner table on a paper and becomes distracted by Thea, who begins imitating him. Ellen spots them in quite an obvious recall to the original where Sean and Martin did the same thing at the dinner table. We find out in the aftermath that this is a regular family trait of the Brody's to imitate each other at the dinner table. The shoe is firmly on the other foot as Thea goes to bed and Ellen tries to have a beer with her son, who tries to shut her down instantly. Ellen once again alludes to the never-ending role of a mother, which comes into play later following the banana boat attack.

Michael is tagging conch near a shipwreck when Jake notifies him that the shark is heading directly for him. This creates minor suspense as we wonder when the shark will appear but when it does the model bumbles from side to side, evaporating any tension that may have previously existed.

As the shark chews the submersible to bits, Michael swims into the nearby shipwreck. Despite my previous criticism of the shark, we have a stunning shot coming up as Small's score blends perfectly with an overhead shot of the shark's silhouette swimming and nearly eclipsing an opening in the ship's roof. Simple but really effective.

Surely there must have been an insistence from Sargent or the producers to show more of the shark because it feels like POV shots would have worked better as it navigated the inside of the wreckage hunting for Michael. The shark's initial attack inside the ship is quite suspenseful as Michael escapes in the nick of time, barging through a locked door.

Jake meanwhile, adhering to his reckless nature wants all of the crew to go down with spears to search and retrieve Michael, whilst staving off a 25 foot Great White. The shark bursts through the adjacent wall to try to get Michael (exposing a pump in the model's mouth in the process) before he manages to escape to the surface.

After another sleepless night, in typical male fashion Michael, against Jake's wishes, wants to go back into the water and get over the shock of the attack. This seems to be going quite well until he is almost attacked by a moray eel. It is also worth noting that this showboating exercise is all happening while Carla's sculpture is being unveiled to the locals by Commissioner Witherspoon (played by the late Melvin Van Peebles).

Louisa remarks about the no-show of Michael and Jake, with Carla palming it off, saying they will be there. Thea has become distracted again and asks if she can go on the banana boat, which is being manned by her friend Margaret and her mother. Ellen, rightfully, is a bit wary at first, but Carla reassures her that they are safe.

Carla is called to the stage but Ellen continues to be more and more agitated, and just as Carla's speech is set to begin Ellen spots the dorsal fin pierce the water trailing the banana boat. Ellen's waddle towards the water is quite comical but Carla's reaction is harrowing as she charges towards the water, screaming for her daughter.

The initial stalking of the banana boat works quite well, but Sargent once again slows everything down as the attack happens with the unfortunate Mrs Ferguson (Stuntwoman Diane Hetfield) becoming the shark's latest dish. Surely this scene would have been more visceral if the attack was quicker, akin to Alex Kittner's attack in the first Jaws; but one can assume that De Guzman and Sargent felt this would be retreading old ground.

Having said this, the slow shot of Mrs Ferguson's corpse being slowly dragged under one final time is quite arresting.

The terror Ellen experienced during this sequence seems to flip on a knife's edge as her mind instantly heads to irrational revenge. After commandeering Michael and Jake's boat Neptune's Folly, she sets off to sea without any real weapons to hunt a 25-foot shark…

In the meantime, Michael has returned to his home to discover that Thea was attacked on the banana boat, which means it's time to confess about tracking the shark. Understandably, Carla absolutely loses it with him, as he asks about Ellen's whereabouts with that Brody intuition that she may have done something reckless.

Tagging Jake along for the ride, Michael teams up with the conveniently-fishing Hoagie, to get him to fly to Ellen's location. Jake finally joins the dots between the shark they are tracking and the banana boat attack, with Hoagie revealing that a shark that killed Martin (when exactly?) and Sean is following the family, which at this stage makes it feel like he has been infected by the temporary insanity of the Brody's. The tone has been moderately serious up until this point, but it feels like this is when Jaws: The Revenge really unravels quickly.

From the air we see the shark approaching Neptune's Folly, with Hoagie's plan to hover above to frighten it? As previously mentioned, this is where the plot becomes quite incoherent, to say the least.

Ellen goads the shark towards her, and when the shark breaches she seems oddly shocked it went for her; I don't really know what she was expecting at this stage.

Hoagie on the other hand is full of bright ideas, deciding to crash land the plane, allowing Michael and Jake to swim to the boat and Ellen. Jake did previously warn Hoagie about the shark being attracted by the electromagnetic of the metal of the plane but he still prances out, rambling as the shark attacks and sinks his plane. Initially, we are led to believe Hoagie has been eaten too but this is another bait and switch, although it doesn't quite top what's to come.

Ellen's reasoning once she is embraced by Michael is, 'there was nothing else to do', which in the Bahamas I find hard to believe. It feels like De Guzman was at a loss to explain this plan in any shape or form except for a means to get us to the final showdown.

Hoagie is revealed to be alive and even though he quips about the shark's breath, it is unclear if he was attacked or not. From here Michael Caine seems to go full rogue and just becomes a caricature either rambling about problems with the boat or telling crap jokes.

Don't worry as Jake has a plan to attach a transmitter to one of his contraptions that will allow them to shock the shark to death from afar. The only dangerous part is getting the transmitter into the shark's mouth first.

Ultimately Jake's plan works but at a cost as he also falls into the shark's mouth as it has now mastered breaching on its tail. Sargent's choice once again to make this scene extra slow motion makes the shark look unbelievably comical and the mute reactions of Michael and Ellen are also rather funny as he is carried off in the shark's mouth still fighting to get free.

Hoagie actually has the most genuine reaction of the group, as he just lowers his head, defeated. After screaming after Jake, Michael snaps out of it and realizes the shark has the transmitter in its gut and starts to shock the shark.

Ellen starts to have flashbacks to scenes she wasn't present for including the finale of Jaws and Sean's death at the start of this film plus the banana boat attack for which she was present. Now steering the boat she is heading directly for the shark, which is being shocked out of the water and begins roaring like a lion for some unknown reason.

Once the shark and the broken bowsprit (from Jake's apparent death) collide, the fish explodes for another unknown reason. The dead shark now sinks to the bottom of the ocean with part of the boat in tow.

Michael, Ellen and Hoagie manage to escape unharmed and in the aftermath, we hear mumbles from afar which turn out to be miraculously resurrected, Jake. Did he creep out of the shark's stomach post-explosion?

Supposedly, test audiences were unhappy with Jake's apparent death which was one of the reasons for the extra scenes being filmed on the Universal sound stage after the film's theatrical release.

The original ending of the film saw the shark pierced with the bowsprit, splitting the boat in half before sinking to the bottom of the ocean, leaving Ellen, Michael and Hoagie as the only survivors.

It is never explained how they get back to shore but we can assume one of Hoagie's co-pilots comes to pick them up.

Ellen offers the Brody's to come to Amity for the summer, where it is safe to say Thea will be staying away from any banana boat rides.

The most surprising thing about Jaws: The Revenge in recap is just how low the body count is, with just two deaths and three fake-out deaths (including Ellen's dream) that are quickly retconned.

Joseph Sargent's plan was to go back to basics, but what we got instead was the most outlandish, bizarre and at times strangely poignant entries in the series.

Alternative Cuts

Hoagie and Ellen talk at Nassau docks in a
deleted scene from Jaws: The Revenge

Alternative and extended cuts of films are often the holy grail for many a film buff, and Jaws: The Revenge happened to have two!

For this chapter, we will take a closer look at the extended cut for AMC plus the botched ratio cut which was screened on the BBC.

The AMC Cut

When feature films had their television debuts, sometimes they would be required to have a minimum runtime of 100 minutes, so the network would be able to run commercial breaks that would ensure it fit comfortably into their schedule.

Jaws 2 (1978) was one of the films that would add in extra or deleted footage to fill its quota for its television debut on TBS. The theatrical version of Jaws 2 was 116 minutes whereas the TBS version is 119 minutes and features five additional scenes.

When it came time for the television debut of Jaws: The Revenge, AMC would once again look to bulk out the runtime to meet the aforementioned criteria – but this time Universal was ready.

During the shoot for 'Revenge' four scenes were shot that ultimately didn't make the final cut.

Here is a breakdown of the scenes and how they fit into the overall narrative for *Revenge* -

During the opening credits, coupled with Michael Small's theme we also get a narration that kicks in once the title card has hit the screen. The voice says,

"Since time immemorial events have taken place with no evident reason for their happening. Such phenomena has been men's dilemma and the subject of constant philosophical discussions. When there is no factor motivating an event, no case of cause creating effect; what triggered the action? Fate or circumstances? What you are about to see concerns such an event. Maybe you can determine here whether we are dealing here with circumstances or fate?"

While this all sounds very serious it comes across like we are set to watch a documentary or found-footage movie, not a shark attack movie. The voiceover work was done by the renowned Canadian actor Percy Rodriguez, who would also go on to lend his talents to the Jaws documentary The Shark Is Still Working in 2005.

The second added sequence takes place as Hoagie and Ellen attend the Bahamas street festival, as Michael and Jake take a day off to jam on Jake's front porch. Jake plays the drums whilst making up lyrics as he goes and Michael strums the guitar.

After singing songs about moray eels and conchs, Michael talks of his guilt for not being there for Carla's sculpture presentation. Weirdly, Jake talks about tracking the shark but because of how it has been edited into the film, the duo hasn't actually encountered the shark for the first time yet, making for a very confusing scene.

In the next sequence, Jake is seen in the yellow submersible as he quips back and forth with Michael on the barge. As Jake discovers a number of conch we cut to an image of the shark on the surface and seemingly swimming towards him. This shot had been seen previously in the making of documentary for WSBK.

We build to Jake's first encounter with the shark as it bumps the side of the submersible but instead of saying, 'Holy shit', Jake says 'Holy cow' instead. As the shark breaches and starts to chew the wooden part of the barge William's dialogue also changed from 'Jesus Christ' to 'Judas Priest'. As the shark descends into the depths we also get an extra shot of its tail and dorsal fin as it goes deeper into the water with cutaways to Ellen paralysed by fear at the carnival.

When Jake, Michael, Carla and Ellen turn up to the New Year's Party at the Casino, we see Jake pointing towards Louisa to ask when she finishes her shift, to which she whispers 'five minutes'. The same as the theatrical cut, Carla notices Hoagie celebrating a win at the table at the far end of the room. As Michael goes to check on their table, Jake, Carla and Ellen go over to investigate.

When the trio arrives at the table, Hoagie wins again and hugs and kisses a random woman in the crowd. This then transcends into the theatrical cut where Hoagie loses after putting everything on the line.

One part of the Bahama's we don't see in the theatrical cut of *Revenge* is the docks where the cruise ships are based. While this is nothing anyone asked for, this added scene attempts to flesh out Ellen and Hoagie's budding relationship. Ellen talks about going home soon and thanks Hoagie for being a good friend. This leads into the scene where they kiss for the first (and only) time.

After sending Thea to bed, Ellen and Michael shoot the breeze in the kitchen. In a strange attempt to get closer to her standoffish son, Ellen threatens to tickle him before telling a pretty awful joke about an Egyptian archaeological dig. This does break the ice with them and make Michael smile but it's safe to say Ellen won't be adorning any comedy clubs any time soon.

The most notorious scene to be added to the AMC broadcast was of course the finale which featured the death of Jake and plenty more shots of the shark stalking Neptune's Folly.

Jake's attack here is much briefer with less blood in the water and no shots of Jake in the shark's mouth as he is dragged under. There are odd POV shots of the shark stalking the boat but because of the rapid cuts the score becomes oddly mixed and seems to flit from dramatic to calm in an instant.

As the boat approaches the shark, Hoagie's dialogue is edited, saying 'Sweet Judas we are heading straight for it', instead of 'Sweet Jesus….'

A number of rapid cuts are now employed with recycled shots of the shark breaching as they get closer and bowsprit looks set to impale the roaring Great White. We see a slow-motion shot of the almost upright shark as the bowsprit impales it through the chest.

There is more roaring as the impaled shark starts to bleed profusely from the mouth and take the ship down with it. We see the shark sink to the bottom attached to part of Neptune's Folly, which broke off during the collision.

After fading to black, we head to Nassau airport where Ellen is heading home, with the line about looking after Jake cut off given he was killed off during this cut of the film.

Weirdly, the AMC cut of the film still clocks in at 91 minutes, which is only one minute more than the theatrical version.

An alternative shot of Jake's death

The BBC Cut

In what was clearly another breakdown in communications between Universal and the BBC, the wrong screen ratio was used for the film's TV debut. This would highlight a number of errors and only add to the film's infamously bad reputation.

Jaws: The Revenge was presented theatrically in Widescreen Cinemascope or 2:35:1 ratio, which is widely considered as the most common presentation for feature films.

Instead of the 2:35:1 ratio, *Revenge* was screened in the 4:3 ratio, which was created with the debut of televisions and allowed viewers to get a full-screen experience and not have any blank spaces.

The first instance where this is glaringly obvious is during the attack of Michael in the submersible by the shark. In the open matte (or 4:3) presentation as the shark grabs onto the submersible the wires on the underside of the shark can clearly be seen.

As the shark pursues Michael towards the shipwreck the wires continue to be visible, which instantly removes any kind of realism from the scene. Even as the shark slinks into the wreckage the wires are still visible on its undercarriage.

Another infamous clanger from this sequence is the air pump that appears to come out of the shark's mouth as it bursts through the wall as Michael escapes. While this was nothing to do with the ratio error, it still shouldn't be shown on a film with a budget of over $20 million.

During the finale of the film, the BBC cut also uses an alternative shot of Jake being grabbed by the shark off the bowsprit after dropping the shock device into its mouth. This shot is from the left and shows more of the shark out of the water with Jake in its jaws.

Unlike the AMC cut, the BBC version also shows Jake struggling with the shark as he is dragged under, alluding to his miraculous survival in other cuts of the film. Once again the mechanical undercarriage can be seen as the shark swims out of shot.

Once pierced with the bowsprit of Neptune's Folly the shark again continues to roar and bleed from the mouth unlike the 'explosion' ending used for the international and DVD versions.

Ellen's line about looking after Jake is also edited out of this version too, as he is presumed dead after being dragged under by the shark before it is speared by the bowsprit.

Another interesting anecdote about the BBC cut of *Revenge* is the reduced run time, with 7 minutes of footage removed leaving it with a runtime of 83 minutes 17 seconds, although a lot of this is sped up or cut credits at the close of the film.

The minor cuts in the film include the initial attack on Sean, slight cuts to the banana boat, although these are not substantial amounts of time.

Scoring Jaws: The Revenge

Jaws: The Revenge was scored by prolific television and film composer Michael Small, best known for his work on Marathon Man (starring Jaws alumni Roy Scheider), The Driver (1978) and The Stepford Wives (1975).

Small had originally planned to score Broadway shows before he ended up writing scores for feature films.

While opinions of the film itself are lukewarm at best, the soundtrack for *Revenge* has garnered admiration with its mix of the familiar with some experimental elements.

Initially MCA Records had planned on an LP release of the score, but after the critical panning this was promptly cancelled.

The first time the score became available to purchase was in 1994, as part of a 2-CD compilation 'Best of Adventure' from Edel, which also featured unreleased scores of The Goonies, Shoot to Kill plus Fandango. This would only be a fraction of the score, clocking in at just 11 minutes that had been re-recorded by the City of Prague Orchestra.

On 16th February 2015 the complete score was finally released by Intrada Records, including one cue of source music and some alternates sourced from the original stereo mixes prepared for the film.

A second release in 2000 featured previously used artwork for Jaws 2, with a shark fin piercing the ocean during a sunset. This was a more stripped-back release with just 28 minutes of music, omitting a number of tracks used in the film.

Here is a breakdown of the 2015 release of the soundtrack, track-by-track -

Main Title – The music starts with a low 'roar' sound and suspenseful strings and brass. As the main titles appear on-screen a triumphant brass fanfare starts before a fast-paced version of the shark theme plays. This quicker version of the familiar John Williams theme is adventurous and menacing before climaxing with the more traditional version of the theme.

This track is intense and showcases Small playing with various sections of the orchestra, creating a sense of urgency and adventure.

Sean Attacked – The attack scene of Sean Brody begins with an ominous two-note shark motif when the shark's POV arrows in on the youngest Brody son. Accelerating, much like the shark, this part of the score alternates between a powerful version of the shark theme and dissonant orchestral outbursts during the brutal attack.

Identification – The music for the scene where Ellen goes to identify her son's remains adds a layer of tragedy to this brief sequence and recalls the discovery of Chrissie's remains from the original Jaws.

Run – Funeral – The melancholic music continues as Michael Brody arrives in Amity and recalls childhood memories of Sean, before switching seamlessly to the funeral sequence where Ellen recalls her deceased son's imitation of his father at the dinner table in Jaws.

Flight to the Bahamas – An unused track has Ellen leaving with Michael's family to the Bahamas. Similar to 'Identification' the sad music continues until the plane arrives in the Bahamas with the score becoming more uplifting.

Ellen Warns – This suspenseful track is used when Ellen spots Thea playing on the docks. Albeit short, Small manages to navigate effortlessly from suspense to regret as Ellen instantly regrets berating her granddaughter. Introducing the sound of electronic echoing bells, this motif will be employed later in the film as Ellen begins to sense the shark's presence.

Ellen's Dream – Considered a highlight of the score, this music starts with some suspense as Michael shows Ellen his wife's sculpture, which resembles a shark's jaws. We then see Ellen swimming in the crystal clear waters off-shore as the tranquil track becomes more menacing and accelerates as we swap the shark POV, which attacks Ellen. The music and the attack scene conclude abruptly as it is revealed to be a nightmare.

Tagging the Conchs – This is basic 'diving music' that was unused, and was showing the underwater activities of Michael Brody and Jake studying sea snails.

Ellen Plays with Leah – Notable for using the incorrect name of Thea Brody, this unused track should have been inserted into the Christmas scene where the youngest Brody quizzes her grandmother about her late uncle. A slower version of the shark theme introduction is playing in the background.

Jaws the Revenge – This track uses music from the Main Titles as the shark is shown swimming menacingly into the Bahamas. Ellen is then shown playing with Thea on the beach, with the shark theme playing as her feet touch the water, with the first use of the 'telepathic' echoing bells motif.

Ellen Flies the Plane – Following a brief introduction the flying theme plays during the scene where Ellen receives piloting lessons from Hoagie. A breezy and light piece of music, this track is also used for the final scene of the film at the airport.

Shark Attacks Jake in Sled – Starting with suspense and the previously established 'roar' effect, this pulsing action track plays as Jake first sees the shark before it breaches to attack the barge. The shark theme then plays as the shark descends back into the water.

Don't Tell Mother – The music starts when Michael asks Jake not to tell Ellen about their encounter with the shark earlier that day. The short track uses the 'telepathic' motif as Michael stares at the ocean.

Saying Goodnight – A delicate short romantic interlude starts with a love scene between Michael and Carla and closes with Hoagie saying goodnight to Ellen. This track shows Small's range and certainly captures the romance implied in both sequences.

Shark Takes Bait – Applying a unique arrangement of the two-note shark theme resembling a march, the rhythm accelerates as we see the shark approaching Michael and Jake's boat as they attempt to start tracking it. Suspenseful music is applied as it breaches and takes the bait before a more action-themed piece followed by a rhythmic percussion before a big stinger as the tagged shark swims away.

Runaway Bay – A light 'Caribbean' source music track plays as Ellen and Hoagie enjoy a drink at a beach bar. An overlong track with no dramatic progression this feels slightly out of place and could have worked better as part of the finale.

Alright Mr. Fish – Michael and Jake continue to track the shark, with the telepathic motif playing as the shark is shown swimming away.

Michael's Dream – A big brass stinger plays as Michael has a nightmare of the shark jumping out of the water, with the music echoing his concerns as he wakes up.

Peek-A-Boo – Mirroring the scene from Jaws, Thea begins to imitate Michael at the dinner table, which is spotted by Ellen. Small opts for a more innocent, warm piece of music, reflecting the gestures being made by Thea.

Picking Up Signals – As Michael continues with the conchs' research the shark approaches, with the shark theme starting to play. Michael boards the submarine as a suspenseful rhythm plays before the telepathic echoing bells motif concludes the track.

Michael Attacked By Shark – One of the most memorable set pieces from *Revenge* was apparently extended after the score was complete with the music looped to cover the increased sequence.

Starting with the fanfare used during the main titles, the shark theme is then used to accentuate the action sequence as Michael is chased through an underwater shipwreck. As he enters the sunken ship the music shifts towards suspense with the shark in pursuit. The final part of the track, which wasn't used in the film, scored Michael's escape to the surface.

Michael At Mirror – Following Michael's attack, the telepathic motif plays before changing to the new 'resolution' theme, which will be used later as Ellen goes out to sea to face the shark.

Moray Eel – The first part of this track wasn't used in the film, as Michael returns to his diving job the day after the attack in the shipwreck. A big stinger is used followed by the new resolution theme as Michael recovers from being scared by a moray eel.

Banana Boat – Possibly the most memorable sequence of the entire film, sees Thea attacked by the shark whilst on a banana boat as Carla's sculpture ceremony takes place on the beach. The telepathic motif is employed again as Ellen starts to feel uneasy as the shark fin rises from the ocean and approaches the banana boat. A fast-paced arrangement of the shark theme used in the main titles plays with the track becoming more intense as the shark devours a woman from the banana boat.

Ellen Goes Out To Sea – After the banana boat attack, Ellen rushes to the dock and takes Michael's boat to go and face the shark at sea. The 'resolution' previously mentioned during Michael's nightmare sequence is played in full as she navigates the boat out to sea. A beautiful and bittersweet track.

Michael Runs For Help – When Michael returns home he learns of Thea's attack and realises his mother and his boat are missing. Small uses an action-themed track to reflect the urgency of the situation as Michael goes to Jake and acquires a small boat to go after her.

Plane Buzzes Shark – We see the shark's POV as it approaches Ellen, with the shark theme arrangement from 'Shark Takes Bait' used. Once Ellen spots the fin approaching in the distance the 'supernatural' shark theme bridge plays in a dramatic statement as woman and fish face off. The action arrangement from the main titles returns as Hoagie spots the shark approaching the boat before it breaches and attacks Ellen.

Is Hoagie Dead? – After the stunt of the plane landing on the water near Neptune's Folly, Michael and Jake swim to the boat. The music swells with suspense as Hoagie starts to leave the plane, before the shark attacks and sinks it. A powerful rendition of the shark theme plays before a tragic piece plays as Ellen, Michael and Jake believe Hoagie to be dead.

Killing of Jake – Jake prepares an electrical transmitter, aiming to shock the shark to death. The shark theme begins again as Michael spots the shark approaching before an aggressive track begins as Jake attempts to feed the transmitter to the shark.

When the shark disappears the music becomes more suspenseful before dissonant music is used as the shark takes the transmitter and Jake into its jaws. As we know this part of the film was edited following test screenings, with Jake surviving the attack and miraculously reappearing after the shark is killed.

Shocked Shark – The Finish – The finale was re-edited heavily after Small completed his score. The original track suggests a more streamlined finale, without the flashbacks to Sean's attack and Brody killing the shark in the first film.

An action rhythm starts when Ellen sees the fin coming towards the boat, with a powerful rendition of the shark theme as she turns the boat towards the shark.

As Ellen impales the prow of the boat into the shark, a big orchestral stinger is played (which is looped twice in the film) before some tranquil music plays. This music runs longer than the finished sequence as a deleted sequence showed Ellen, Hoagie and Michael in the water after the shark is killed.

The final scene of the movie shows Ellen boarding a plane with Hoagie, leaving the Bahamas. The flying theme returns with the main title fanfare closing the score as the plane flies into the sunset.

Jaws The Revenge – End Credits – A looped version of the Main Titles music, this is a more traditional take on the Jaws theme. Small's vision was to bring the series full circle with the first movie's theme closing *Revenge*.

Flight to the Bahamas (alternate take) – Although billed as an alternate take, this track has no significant differences to the one used in the film.

Shark Attacks Jake In Sled (alternate take) – The difference with this track is in the electronics used and the beginning of the track.

Banana Boat (original ending) – This alternate track uses a big crescendo ending, which was replaced by a more subdued finale in the film version.

Music producer Douglass Fake revealed more about the scoring experience for Small and explained why some of the score went unused.

"Several cues were dialled out before completion. Some were dropped entirely; still, others were simply re-tracked into scenes for which they weren't originally intended. The opening of the 'Main Title' and portions of 'Sean Attacked' were tracked into other scenes, the second half of 'Michael Runs for Help' was trimmed and both print takes of 'Flight to the Bahamas' and 'Ellen Plays with Thea' went unused," he revealed.

"But the most egregious changes to Small's score involved the problematic finish to the film and its abrupt climax – which required numerous edits and trims to the music during post-production."

Film Score magazine reviewed Small's score for Jaws: The Revenge in their August 2000 issue, giving it three stars out of five. The reviewer A.K.B notes,

"Small still gave *Revenge* a lot more than it deserved – and this is a much better score than *Deep Blue Sea*…whatever that means. It's sad that the great Michael Small was delegated utter garbage like Jaws: The Revenge in the late 80s – and even worse that he has yet to find his way back to the material he deserves."

Starlog Magazine #320 in March 2004, would feature Small in its The Last Farewells feature, acknowledging his work on *Revenge* plus The Lathe of Heaven (1980) and The Stepford Wives (1975), following his passing in the previous November from cancer.

Film Score magazine would also feature a posthumous tribute to Michael Small, who also adorned their front cover, for their September 2005 issue.

The 9-page feature entitled The Poet of Paranoia, is a fascinating insight into Small's work, with interviews with his widow Lynn and long-time collaborator Christopher Dedrick, who also orchestrated the score for *Revenge*.

Speaking about collaborating with Small, Dedrick commented,

"To my view, there was true genius in his ability to find the notes that not only worked with the picture, but added, lifted, deepened, accented, blended…did whatever was needed to make the very most of the moment. And always in context of the greater arc of score and film.

"Michael's attention to tempo and pace was also very instructive to me. After improvising to a scene and playing with various tempi, he would choose a click and then often leave the metronome clicking away the whole time he was composing. There was no way he was going to get in front of the orchestra and discover that the tempo wasn't quite right—an experience that is only too common in less prepared situations. Another aspect of his attention to rhythm showed up in his constant use of meter changes, aggravating to his copyists, but essential to his style."

Joseph Sargent reflects on Revenge

Joseph Sargent on set of Jaws: The Revenge

Joseph Sargent was interviewed by the Television Academy Foundation about his career in film and television before he passed away in 2014.

Surprisingly Sargent was quite candid about the experience of working on Jaws: The Revenge.

"Sid Sheinberg's mandate was to find a way to kill the shark in a different way; that hasn't been done before because the shark needed to be killed at the end of the movie.

"The trouble with a franchise is that unlike the original, which of course, burst on the screen with such impact and such dynamics and was such a brilliant film – everything that follows can't help but be a pale reflection of the original impact no matter how threatening you make the shark. No matter how clever a device for killing him, no matter what you do it's only a second, pale nothing compared to the original," Sargent explained.

Speaking about his relationship with Sheinberg, he noted,

"We toyed with the idea of 'where can we go with this?' So Sid seduced me completely into the deal by making me the director and the executive producer and I could call all the shots, hire the writer, hire the crew; do everything – it was my baby. How do you walk away from something like that?"

"Even though I knew this was enemy territory, that there was disaster as a possibility I was still fired up – the thought that I was my own boss.

Sargent said the decision to add a more supernatural element to the Jaws mythos simply came out of desperation.

"We tried something that evidently came out of desperation to find something fresh to do with the shark. Now, what can that be? We thought maybe if we take a mystical point of view and go for a little bit of magic we might be able to find something interesting to sit through. So what could that be? The shark comes in and attacks the younger son of the Roy Scheider character, who was killed in a previous attack, so the mother now is convinced that the shark is out to get revenge.

"It's a preposterous premise but at the time we were kind of fired up by the possibilities of okay, it's a stretch but it may set off some sparks and Sid Sheinberg was thrilled with it. He said this sounds like a good, fresh way to go about it, thank you very much, go on.

"We developed it on the basis that everybody was excited about the possibilities that a shark could wreak vengeance for (the) killing of his cousins, or whatever they were.

"It's amazing when you make a choice artistically despite whatever sophistication, whatever professionalism you've achieved by that time, you can fall into a sort of romantic love affair with a notion that is so far out that it actually feels right or feels challenging. We felt that way and thought this just might work, now came the question – how do we kill the shark?"

The decision to shoot in the Bahamas came from the script, according to Sargent, plus he wanted to shoot in this location.

"First of all, we decided to shoot in Martha's Vineyard because that's where it all started and that's where the kid gets killed. So she (Ellen) moves out of there, to the Bahamas because I was allowed to choose any location I wanted, plus we had written it that way. Because, why not? Let's shoot in the Bahamas.

"What's down there? The older son (Michael) who is a marine biologist and you can already sense where this is going. The shark is after the family, but great whites don't operate in warm water which makes everyone feel safe.

"Ellen moves down there with her grief and meets Michael Caine who surprisingly thought it was a good script too. The rest is history. The shark does in fact follow them down to the Bahamas and tries to kill the son and the mother and struggle, struggle, struggle and the front of the boat is steered by the mother, this stiletto-like boat and impales the shark and that does the shark in," Sargent continued.

Sargent looked back on the experience with a wink and a smile, more in disbelief that the concept got beyond pre-production.

"How do grown men with rather good credentials in terms of their training, their worldliness, how do we get involved with something like that idiotic?

"It still puzzles me. I have formed all kinds of rationales about how we can get trapped like that and some of them were probably worth listening to. For instance, you think it is a great, fresh approach and you want it to be, you want it to work and you blackout (the negatives). Sid wanted it to work, I did, Michael Caine did, everyone involved with the production did. There was one descending voice that said ahead of time that this is not gonna work, this is too silly."

The Novelisation

Former Naval Aviator and Scuba Diver turned Author Hank Searls returned to the Jaws franchise to pen the novelisation of Jaws: The Revenge, having previously released a novel of Jaws 2 in April 1978, based upon the original script by John D. Hancock.

Searls' novel for *Revenge* would aim to plug some of the plot holes of Michael De Guzman's script and establish a more cohesive plot.

The Akron Beacon Journal's Bill O'Connor interviewed Searls about the novelisation, with the author saying,

"The movie (Jaws) is so popular because there is a monster, maybe, inside all of us. As long as the water is clear, we can handle it. The murky water hides the thing."

The Herald Statesman talked to Searls about the novelisation, with the article published on the same day as the film's theatrical release (17th July).

"You don't have to exaggerate a shark," Searls commented.

"The Great White is an eating machine, the most efficient predator the world has ever known,"

Searls was also interviewed by Steve Bornfield of the Poughkeepsie Journal on 19th July, just two days after the nationwide release of Jaws: The Revenge to discuss the recently released novelisation that hit bookshelves on 1st July.

"The shark calls on something in the subconscious, that is eternal, a primordial fear, this monster in murky water that might come up and devour you," Searls said.

"The book is a much more intimate experience and it can be more exciting. That menacing shark is, to me, more exciting than the one on the screen, because this is happening within your head. You may not hear the music, but I'm often more in suspense from the written word.

Discussing the glaring plot hole of the psychic shark, Searls notes,

"Somehow, the shark knows she (Ellen Brody) is in the Bahamas. That's something you can do in a novel. Even though a shark is an insensitive animal with a fist-sized brain, by the time an author gets through with it, if properly done, you will believe this spell is cast and that the shark has a spiritual grudge against Ellen.

The author also briefly discusses the introduction of voodoo priest Papa Jacques, who controls the actions of the shark for a large chunk of the novelisation.

"In the book, I don't contend that the shark is thinking at all. That's why I've got the voodoo guy standing in for him. He thinks he's possessed by the shark, a living, breathing epitome of sharkdom on dry land. He does a lot for the book, but he would have been corny in the movie.

"This shark is related to the first one. It's a whole family, and they all hate the Brody's. This time it's personal," he concluded.

Joel Achenbach's regular feature in The Miami Herald took aim at the novelisation of Jaws: The Revenge in the 9th August edition, calling it 'the literary equivalent of a sausage', when discussing the struggles of lesser authors to get noticed with publishers at Random House.

Author Dan West reviewed the novelisation of Revenge for HorrorNovelReviews.com, saying,

"With Jaws The Revenge, author Hank Searls accomplishes one thing, and that thing is proving that you just can't polish a turd."

Author and screenwriter Matt Serafini also reviewed the book for Dread Central and was slightly more positive with his post.

"Searls is an excellent writer and Jaws The Revenge is a fast-moving and vivid read. It was never a good idea to grant supernatural abilities to the great white, but this is a superior iteration of the story. Far more enjoyable than what Joseph Sargent gave us during the summer of 1987," Serefini commented.

Writing for The Omniplex website, Austin Shinn also praised Searls' work, saying,

"Searls fleshes everything out and gives every character motivation. He also has a good eye for scene and detail. There's a clear portrait of what's going on in this book which I read before watching the film. It's definitely a brisk moving book.

"This is a silly, absurd ride but it ain't dull. Had this been the film, hell we might've gotten Jaws 5. It's just that much fun."

Cassandra Rose reviewing the book for Bibliomantics said,

"Jaws: The Revenge: it's a tale as old as time. Man kills the shark. Man kills a different shark. Possible descendent of deceased sharks follow the man's family to the Bahamas and begins systematically killing them.

"You know, that old story.

In an attempt to fix the many problems with the film, author Hank Searls (the "nationwide #1 bestselling author of Jaws 2") makes things even worse, with a story that doesn't feature a shark killing anyone between pages 14 and 240, a bizarre story about the cartel and that major plot point: voodoo."

PopOptiq.com's Kenny Hedges was minorly complimentary of the novelisation, commenting,

"...the novelization at least tries, however ineptly, to create some tension with Gary's shark sense tingling and ludicrous, unrelated subplots."

Tyler Liston, writing for the Nightmare on Film Street site commented,

"While the novel isn't necessarily good, it does give us a few nuggets of gold that make it the infinitely superior version of Jaws: The Revenge."

Regardless of the whacky plot and polarising reviews, Hank Searls' Jaws: The Revenge novelisation remains a highly sought after collector's item for fans of the Jaws series.

Digesting Jaws The Revenge by Hank Searls

Hank Searls' novelisation opens with a quote from Joseph Conrad's short novel Typhoon from 1902, reading -

"The sea never changes and its works, for all the talk of men, are wrapped in mystery."

There is also a quote from Richard Ellis' The Book of Sharks, which explains how sharks have electrical and chemical receptors unequaled in the animal kingdom; which potentially alludes to the voodoo elements of this story.

We learn in the opening paragraphs that our shark is 28 feet long and has come to feed in Amity after being drawn by 'random impulses' from Montauk Point. This hungry male makes quick work of a baby seal and its mother for good measure, as they try to escape onto a buoy.

Switching attention to Ellen Brody, she visits her son Sean, and we find out this will be her first Christmas without 'Marty'. Interestingly, Ellen also refers to 'The Troubles' describing the events of both Jaws and Jaws 2, even though Revenge was pitched initially as a straight sequel to the original film. This was perhaps Searls taking creative liberties, having not wanted to write out his own novelisation of Jaws 2.

There is a great callback to Jaws when Ellen thinks about Sean following in Martin's footsteps to become part of the Amity Police Department, making sly reference to the imitation as first witnessed in the iconic dinner table scene from Jaws.

We discover that the two attacks from the first two films have crippled Amity's economy, as the town prepares for the Christmas pageant. Sean has sent Polly (the receptionist) home to wrap Christmas presents and thus receives the call at the office (with Ellen present) about a wood pile drifting in the channel. Ellen is already manifesting an almost psychic ability that something is off without being able to articulate it, which is a departure from the film where she only seems to connect to the danger once Michael is confronted by the shark on the barge later on.

The rest of this chapter plays out similar to the film as Sean goes to inspect the drifting wood but this time he gets his hand caught on a rusty nail which traps him when the shark attacks. There is no mention of ripping his arm off but we do learn shortly after that the shark bit a large chunk of his torso away plus parts of the boat and a fire extinguisher.

Tiffany, at home with Ellen, asks for stories about her fiance, with Ellen recalling the tale of Sammy the Seal, where Sean attempted to nurse a seal back to health in the Brody garage, much to his father's annoyance. Following this story, Ellen gets an extreme sense that something is wrong and they both go to the harbour and ask the local fishermen to go out and check on Sean.

Tiffany passes out in the car, but Ellen wakes up in the morning to see the fishermen bringing what's left of Sean back to shore.

Michael, Carla and Thea arrive in Amity and as an alternative to the film, they are greeted at the door by Ellen who is barely keeping it together. Much like the film, Ellen tries to stay strong throughout Sean's funeral but leaves before the end of the ceremony. She takes off to the beach nearby and shoots six bullets into the water, as a form of catharsis. What she doesn't know is the shark is still circling the nearby waters and starts to head towards the shoreline and Ellen.

Significantly, we also learn at this point that the shark is a child of the sharks from the first two films, and was part of a school of another male and three female great whites.

A few days later Ellen heads for Nassau and catches a flight with Hoagie, who meets her at the airport for the connection to the

Bahamas from Amity. We also meet Papa Jacques for the first time, as he attempts to catch a lift with Hoagie back to the island. At first, the pilot refuses, but Ellen talks him around. The shark is now also en-route to the Bahamas but first grabs a snack on a dying sperm whale, which had previously been harpooned.

Thea greets her grandmother at Nassau airport and Michael also confronts Papa Jacques, who we find out has a complicated past with the Brody's. Hoagie describes Jacques as a 'Houngan Witch Doctor', and someone not to be trusted.

On the ride back from the airport their taxi is followed by two men on motorcycles who start to shoot at the windows, trying to get to Hoagie. Luckily no one is hurt, and they reach the Brody house where we are introduced to Jake and his wife Louisa, who we find out is also a 'white witch'.

We discover that local drug dealer Rico Lomas put the hit out on Hoagie by the men on the motorcycles, with his next plan to shoot down the pilot's plane.

Michael gets back to the day job, looking for conches in the pink (not yellow) submersible whilst being harassed by Jake on the intercom system. We get the first mention of the BPST (Battery Powered Sonic Transmitter) which will come into play later in the story. Jake also reveals that Michael was a risky hire for the project, given the islanders' views on hiring a 'white'.

In more foreshadowing, Michael is also tempted to explore the shipwreck, where he will be chased later on by the shark.

Back on shore Carla and Ellen attempt to bond over talk of her sculpture, which replaces the scene where Ellen finds the 'shark like' sculpture in the film in Carla's workshop.

The shark continues its journey towards Nassau and is spotted by a drunken newscaster who is fishing off the coast of Nassau.

While the harbinger of doom heads towards the Brody's, they celebrate Christmas Day with Thea getting a number of presents, including one from Uncle Sean. Like the film, Thea asks if Ellen ever disciplined her youngest son, but she answers after recollecting a story from years past while Michael goes silent, holding in his pent up grief for his brother.

Ellen, Thea and Deenie, one of the four children of Jake and Michael's shipmate Clarence, head to the beach to build sandcastles, using her present from Sean.

Deenie brings up the subject of Papa Jacques, who she says could perform a spell that could bring Sean back from the 'waters of the dead'. Before this goes any further Hoagie flies in and drops a mysterious white package nearby, which is collected by an unidentified man who then disappears. Thea notices this and goes looking for it but starts to develop a sickness soon after vomiting three times before Ellen can get her granddaughter home. Is Papa Jacques working against the Brody's?

Thea is now bedridden and a heavy storm has grounded the planes and boats, with Michael setting off to try to find a doctor in a local tourist hotel. Hoagie has arrived to comfort Ellen and they have a similar conversation to the movie about Sean's death and Ellen believing their family is cursed.

Carla meanwhile has become stranded with her agent and decides to have a flutter in the local casino as she waits to get home. Ellen asks for Louisa's help, and she performs a spell that will rid Thea of her illness. At this point, Papa Jacques turns up at the Brody house after Thea called for him but he is ushered away by a returning Michael.

The next day Jake decides to go diving instead of Michael after Louisa warns against it. The shark goes for Jake and then pivots towards the barge with a scene mirroring the film where it takes a big bite out of it, trying to reach Michael. Shaken after the attack, Michael shares the story of Brody and the sharks with his colleagues.

Jake and Michael now begin plans to tag and study the shark but this plan is thrown into chaos when Michael is attacked in the submersible and he becomes trapped in the ship wreckage nearby (again mirroring the film). After hearing that Michael has become trapped, Jake sets out to try and rescue him but the remaining Brody son escapes using his oxygen tank to reach the surface, with the shark still stuck in the wreckage.

Following the attack, the crew begin chumming for the shark and Clarence says that Papa Jacques has cursed their boat. The shark surfaces and Michael manages to attach the tracker but he feels an odd connection with the fish, stating it felt 'it had tagged him too'.

Hoagie's story becomes slightly more clear when it is revealed that he had a daughter who disappeared which caused the breakdown of his marriage. More about this later…

He continues to pursue Ellen and plans a date at Ricardo Lomas' club. This infuriates the club owner who starts to plan his assassination of Hoagie while Ellen tries to find out his true intentions for this date. We later see Hoagie performing what looks like a drug deal outside of his apartment, after it is advised they don't fly home tonight because of the weather.

Papa Jacques continues to be up to no good as he meets his followers at Masthead Point and performs a ritual dance and curses a stolen shirt of Michael's with his shark tooth medallion. Thea, now fully recovered, begins to sleepwalk towards Papa Jacques' location.

Lomas' henchmen Carlos and Alejandro are planning to shoot down Hoagie's plane as he returns to the mainland with Ellen, but after being seen by Michael and Jake they crashland on the beach just feet away from Thea who is building sandcastles. This is a noticeable change in pace for Searls with stakes raised considerably but the shark not really playing a massive part in it.

Ellen is thrown from the plane as she frantically searches for Thea. As Michael arrives to take them all back home, he and Hoagie have a private conversation where he reveals he has seen them chumming for the shark. Michael offers him a deal, saying if he keeps his mouth shut about the shark he won't tell anyone about Hoagie dealing drugs on the island.

In the aftermath of the plane shooting Carlos is double crossed by Lomas and is executed on a boat offshore of Masthead Cay. The sound of the gunshots alerts the shark which begins making its way towards them and devours the corpse of Carlos. Lomas is frantically trying to escape on a jet ski which doesn't work so he starts to swim to shore with the shark in pursuit. He instructs his men to shoot at the ocean and ward off the shark, which allows him to reach the shore unharmed.

Despite their 'deal', Mike tells Ellen about Hoagie's drug pushing activities, whilst Romeo tells Hoagie about Lomas' encounter with the Great White. Hoagie is now planning his endgame to take down Lomas once and for all.

Alejandro notices Hoagie in Lomas' bar and considers shooting him but first notifies Lomas, who has been drunk and coked up to the eyeballs since the incident with the shark, his pride clearly wounded. Lomas invites Hoagie into his office where an intense meeting takes place and it very much feels like whoever draws first will kill the other. Hoagie goads Lomas and blackmails him, effectively telling him he will share his encounter with his counterparts unless he stops dealing on the island immediately.

We revert back to the voodoo side plot as Louisa seeks out Papa Jacques on a hunch and discovers him at Clarence's house where he is performing a spell for Thea, which he completes by biting the head off a live chicken!

The spell begins to take hold as Thea is drawn to the beach to look for her bucket but she is drawn into the ocean, with Ellen going after her.

Mike goes to Clarence's house to investigate and we discover that Clarence's daughter Deenie stole Thea's sand bucket to be part of the ritual by Papa Jacques. The ceremony is still going on but Mike sneaks and destroys Jacques' Asson rattle and then escapes with Louisa.

It is now a race against time for the group, including Carla, to rescue Thea as the shark approaches.

The next day is the Annual Island Festival but Hoagie has other plans as he meets Alejandro to set up a deal. Alejandro threatens to kill all of the Brody's for Lomas if the deal goes awry.

Because we haven't had a shark attack in a while the Great White hunts and devours a windsurfer for a light snack.

Romeo, as well as being a taxi driver is also a part-time Undertaker, with Hoagie looking to set up a final showdown in the funeral parlour with Lomas.

As Carla stresses about her sculpture presentation, in another deviation from the film, Mike tells her about the shark, which does nothing for her stress levels. Meanwhile, Papa Jacques summons the shark to the shore for another feed.

We now find out that Hoagie is an undercover agent and his operation has been going on for 12 months, luring Lomas to Whiskey Cay to stop his drug pushing operation.

In the funeral parlour's embalming lab a secret agent surprises Lomas and it turns into a shootout but the dealer manages to escape into a back alley with a child as a hostage.

Returning to a more familiar plot, Carla's presentation begins and Thea, despite the revelations about the shark, is allowed to go on the banana boat. Mike meanwhile is getting pretty drunk over the road, but when Carla reveals she knew about the heart monitor on the boat Mike begins to panic and channels his inner Martin Brody to clear the water immediately, sensing the shark is near.

Mike, Carla, Jake and Louisa now head for the water to try to stop the banana boat, but they fail and Ellen sees the shark fin approaching the boat. For such an iconic scene within the film, Searls skips over this attack quite quickly, with Margaret De Lacy, the wife of the local dentist, being devoured quite quickly with no real details given.

In the aftermath of this very public attack, Ellen goes with the family to the clinic but then inexplicably disappears to plot her own endgame with the shark.

Lomas hides in the hangar housing Hoagie's plane and after Mike and Jake find out Ellen has 'borrowed' Neptune's Folly they ask Hoagie to fly them out to get her. What they don't know is that Lomas has hidden in the back of the plane and after surprising the trio he demands at gunpoint, to be taken to Spanish Galleon Cay.

Ellen, clad only in her swimsuit, addresses her mad plot subconsciously to kill the shark or potentially turn the gun on herself if she can't get the job done.

The plane has now found Ellen but Lomas is causing chaos up above as he is shot by Jake and ends up falling out of the plane into the ocean as Hoagie tries to hit the shark with the plane – seriously. The shark it seems is trying to sink the ship and breaks the bowsprit in a foreshadowing of its own fate.

Not knowing the severity of the situation, Ellen offers Lomas a lifeline to the boat but the shark gets to him before he can reach the boat. As Lomas is being devoured, Hoagie crashlands the plane and Mike and Jake swim to Neptune's Folly.

Back on the island, Papa Jacques has become quite ill and looks to be nearing death as he tries to guide the shark with the help of a Dambullah African Serpent God.

After prepping the shock machine Jake falls into the water and is seemingly killed off-screen, with no real description. Much the same as one of the film's conclusion's Mike is able to shock the shark to a point where it can be impaled by the broken bowsprit. At the point of death for the shark, Papa Jacques also dies.

To wrap things up, Ellen has a heart-to-heart with Louisa who is mourning the death of Jake but is also planning to go off and begin training to be a nurse. Nothing like a fresh start I suppose.

Instead of returning to Amity, Ellen agrees to a trip to Jamaica with Hoagie as they fly off into the sunset, their troubles now behind them.

As you can see Searls very much attempts to create his own narratives here with introductions of Papa Jacques, Lomas and his goons plus more fleshed out roles for characters such as Hoagie, Louisa, Clarence and Romeo. Whether this works is quite questionable but this novelisation certainly does make for an interesting 'What If?' in the Jaws universe if nothing else.

The Tragedy of Judith Barsi

"I know she is happy, and she doesn't have to live with any more fears and tears. Just remember Judy as the beautiful girl she was." – Agi Barsi (Judith's half-sister)

The most tragic element in chronicling the story of Jaws: The Revenge has definitely been researching the death of Judith Barsi just a year after the film was released, in a double murder-suicide from her father Jozsef, who also killed her mother and then himself.

Barsi's career was set to go on to a whole new level following *Revenge*, as she had already supplied her voice to classics animated features All Dogs go to Heaven and The Land Before Time.

Discovered at the age of five at an ice rink, this led to the young actress earning up to $100,000 a year allowing her family to move to a 3-bedroom house in the West Hills area of Hollywood in 1985.

The first formal abuse claims were filed by her mother Maria in December 1986 to police, claiming her father had threatened to kill her plus choking and hitting her in the face. When police found no evidence of the abuse Maria declined to prosecute.

Before Judith left for the Bahamas to film Jaws: The Revenge she was allegedly threatened by her father with a knife, and he told her this chilling warning,

"If you decide not to come back, I will cut your throat."

Barsi's agent also witnessed Jozsef telling Judith,

"Remember what I told you before you left."

When Judith returned two months later the abuse, unfortunately, continued, with the poor little girl so stressed about this living hell she found herself in that she plucked out her eyelashes and cat's whiskers.

Friends had claimed that Judith had complained about her home life, saying,

"I'm afraid to go home. My daddy is miserable. My daddy is drunk every day, and I know he wants to kill my mother."

Neighbours told the LA Times after the horrific incident that Jozsef had claimed he wanted to kill his wife on multiple occasions and would also claim he would kill his daughter too.

In May 1988 Judith's agent Ruth Hansen started to see the full extent of the abuse her client was receiving at home. Barsi was scheduled for an audition but began crying hysterically and could not talk, so Ruth suggested that she see a psychologist.

The psychologist reported Judith's case to social services, who were also informed by Maria that she planned to begin divorce proceedings soon and move out of their family home.

Maria began to put space between her and her husband, moving into a rented apartment where she and Judith would spend their days before returning to their home at night. Maria's plan was to move on the weekend of 30/31 July, but sadly Jozsef's evil plan was realised before this could happen.

Jozsef had begun drinking heavily, unable to share in his daughter's success. He regularly threatened to kill himself, and after Judith and her mother tried to leave the country he shot her on 25th July 1988 and her mother Maria before shooting himself in their garage.

In the aftermath of the murder-suicide, neighbour Adrienne Conway told the Great Fall Tribune's 28th July 1988 edition,

"She was adorable...quite precocious, blonde and blue-eyed."

It was widely reported across a number of publications that both the bodies of Judith and Maria were set on fire following their deaths by gunshot, with the fires from the bodies causing the windows of the home to explode which alerted neighbours to the incident.

Police Lieutenant Warren Knowles told the Scrantonian Tribune that Jozsef Barsi had shot his wife and daughter in the head before pouring a flammable liquid on them, setting them on fire before shooting himself in the garage.

Chris Daly, a contractor whose mother Eunice lived next door to the Barsi's, told the Herald Examiner that Maria had told numerous people about her plans to divorce Jozsef.

"She said that he threatened to kill both of them and burn the house down if she left. She had been moving her stuff out in boxes. She took the threat seriously. She was scared to death." Daly said.

Eunice also told journalist Michael Fleeman that she first noticed the smoke coming from the Barsi home and feared the worst.

"My first thought as I ran to dial 911 was 'He's done it. He's killed them and set fire to the house, just like he said he would'", she said.

Speaking to the Tallahassee Democrat (29th July 1988), Eunice explained more about the dark nature of Jozsef leading up to the incident.

"She (Maria) told me her husband had been an alcoholic for 30 years. He had threatened to kill both of them and burn the house down. I was afraid," Eunice said.

Eunice Daly also gave a brief insight into the abuse that Judith was suffering from her father.

"He also slapped Judith. Once he yanked her ponytail so hard she flew off her feet," she told the 16th August edition of Globe Magazine.

In the aftermath, it was revealed that Jozsef had been arrested on 20th February 1988 for drink driving and was awaiting trial on 13th September. Another unverified source claimed that Jozsef had been arrested again for drink driving in the interim and had a court appearance scheduled for around the time he executed his wife and daughter, and himself.

An article in The Ukiah Daily Journal on 4th August 1988, featured a quote from Judith's agent Ruth Hansen, claiming more could have been done to prevent this tragedy.

"I believe someone should have checked on this story and saved a child's life," Hansen said.

Judith's funeral took place on Tuesday 9th August 1988 at the Forest Lawn Memorial Park in Los Angeles, buried alongside her mother Maria.

Around 75 friends and relatives attended, including Judith's friend Shawn Samson, who told the Los Angeles press,

"I didn't know a dad could do such a thing to a daughter and a wife."

Agi Barsi, Judith's half-sister also disclosed that Jozsef had previously been abusive to her and that he was a ticking time bomb.

"I lived with my dad, and he did the same things to me that he did to her. It was going to happen sooner or later," Agi said.

Agi also offered this final, heartbreaking note about her half-sister,

"I know she is happy, and she doesn't have to live with any more fears and tears. Just remember Judy as the beautiful girl she was."

Patty Turner, a friend of Maria Barsi told Deidre Phillips, working as part of the Los Angeles press,

"I know that things were extremely bad. The husband gave me chills. I wouldn't go in the house. The cold attitude he had was very unfriendly."

Bonnie Gold of the Harry Gold Talent Agency paid this tribute to Judith in the Winnipeg Free Press,

"She was an incredible, bright, open, loving child. If you saw her you wanted to put your arms around her.

"You read about these things, but you don't expect them to happen to people you know. I think of her as a beautiful young girl who had her life ahead of her."

Her on-screen father in *Jaws: The Revenge*, Lance Guest, would be one of the pallbearers at her funeral. The Gold sisters, Tracey, Missy and Brandy (best known for childhood roles in television series such as Benson, Growing Pains and Baby Makes Five) read the Edgar Guest poem A Child of Mine as part of Judith's eulogy.

Judith's and Maria's bodies were buried on a site overlooking the film and television studios in Burbank.

Although not present at the funeral, *Revenge* co-star Michael Caine paid tribute to Barsi in Hello magazine, saying,

"She was a very talented actress and a lovely young girl."

On 13th August 1988, more dark details emerged from the case with one of Jozsef's former work colleagues Peter Kivlen telling the Tallahassee Democrat that 'Joe', as he called him, had told him 500 times that he was going to kill his wife.

"I'd try to calm him down. I'd tell him 'If you kill her, what will happen with your little one?' I gotta kill her too he responded."

John Johnson reported for the Los Angeles Times (17th August 1988 edition) that a watchdog agency had requested that the child abuse files on Judith Barsi from the Los Angeles County Department of Children's Services be opened to assist with their investigation.

Johnson stated that according to sources, the case without informing the psychologist who was treating Judith for distress; was being linked to the alleged abuse.

The social care worker who was dealing with the Barsi case went into seclusion immediately after the deaths, according to associates.

On 6th September 1988, a Los Angeles county panel revealed that an investigation into threats of violence in the family of Judith Barsi was dropped prematurely due to a lack of resources in the Children's Services department.

After reviewing the confidential files of the investigation, the Commission of Children's Services recommended that the department become more sensitive to the impact of domestic violence on children and look to develop clearer guidelines for closing an inquiry.

During this meeting of the commission, Robert L. Chaffee, Director of the Department for Children's Services, defended his department's handling of the case, saying Maria Barsi had given the impression she had everything under control and wanted the case closed. Whether this was true or a front put on by Mrs Barsi we shall never know.

Helen A. Klein, a member of Children's Services, stated that the reason the county did not act was that Judith was suffering from emotional abuse, not physical abuse.

"Emotional abuse potentially can be as threatening to a child as physical abuse. This is part of the whole problem. It's easy to focus on physical abuse because we can see it," said Klein.

Commission Chairwoman Nancy L. Daly also disclosed that Barsi family friends had informed Children's Services that the state Department of Labor Services, who supervised Judith whilst filming, had seen signs that she was emotionally distressed but never informed county authorities.

It was reported on 8th November 1988 that changes be made to the County Children's Services department following an investigation into the death of Judith Barsi. The department had looked into the case previously but closed it in June when the social worker was assured that both Judith and her mother were moving to another property.

As we know now, just a few short weeks later the entire Barsi family was dead. The panel recommended a lighter caseload for overburdened social workers employed by Children's Services.

Commissioner Stacey Winkler told the hearing that the worker dealing with the Barsi case was also dealing with 67 other cases, with the recommended caseload being a maximum of 39 under a union contract. Any social worker with a higher caseload than 39 would therefore not be subject to discipline for routine infractions.

Department officials defended their handling of the Barsi case, with spokesman Emery Bontrager saying that both the child and the mother were interviewed, with Maria seeming to have everything under control.

Tragically, Judith's other half-sibling Barna would pass away on 3rd March 1995, after drowning in a canal in Scotsdale, Arizona, after battling alcoholism most of his life.

In 2020 the murder-suicide of Judith and Maria was brought back into the public spotlight again, as their former house featured on episodes 10,11 and 12 of the first season of the television series Murder House Flip. Pitched as True Crime meets Fixer Upper, this episode follows the Bernal family who moved into the Barsi house in 2001, not knowing about its dark past.

Things took a supernatural turn as Gaby, daughter of the Bernal family, told her parents she had made an imaginary friend, Joseph (the same name as Jozsef Barsi). For the next ten years since they moved Gaby would have trouble sleeping, having never been able to face the window whilst sleeping, as this was the same position Judith was killed in the same room in 1988.

The renovators from Murder House Flip set about removing the 'bad energy' in the house, which includes new carpeting, decor, furniture and a new garden. Designers Mitch Welch and Joelle Uzyel also gifted the Bernal family purple amethyst crystal, known to promote healing, to keep in Gaby's bedroom.

During this retrospective of Jaws: The Revenge, we will reflect on Judith's contribution to the franchise and wonder what heights she may have gone on to have achieved.

She was involved in one of the most talked-about scenes in the series; the banana boat attack in the Bahamas, as one of the mum's, pulls her from certain death from the marauding Great White and the unfortunate Mrs Ferguson is attacked and dragged to a watery grave.

While Judith's career and life were cut so heartbreakingly short, she will always be remembered by fans of Jaws: The Revenge, All Dogs Go To Heaven and The Land Before Time.

R.I.P Judith Barsi (1978-1988)

Jaws the NES Game

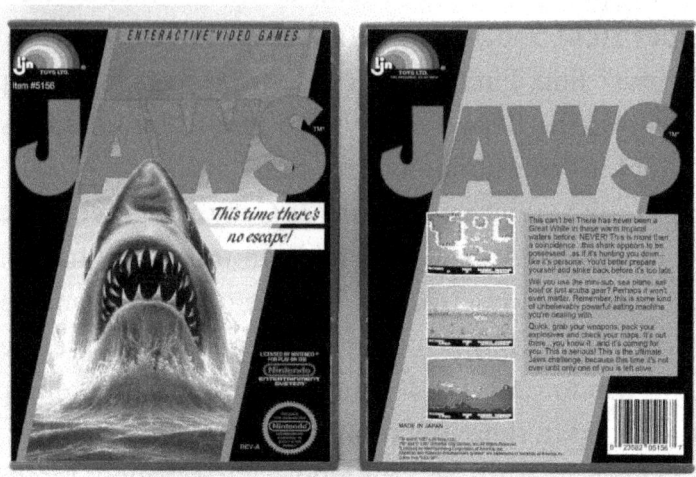

Jaws the Game, released for the NES

Japanese NES game developers Atlus with the help of Westone Bit Entertainment developed Jaws for publishers LJN; with a late 1987 release eyed to coincide with the theatrical release of Jaws: The Revenge.

The box art closely resembles that of Revenge, with its back cover mentioning 'like its personal', echoing the sequel's tagline 'This Time It's Personal'.

Music for Jaws was composed by Shinichi Sakamoto, who only riffs on John Williams' iconic score for the title-screen track. Sakamoto's work uses a change of volume as a way to mimic the movement of water. The overwater music sways from soft to loud and loud to soft, rocking back and forth like the undulating waves of shark-infested waters.

Gameplay-wise, the player pilots a boat across the area, and randomly encounters a group of hostile sea creatures. When the boat hits something in the overhead map the player's perspective changes to a side-view and you are released as a diver who must battle undersea threats such as jellyfish, rays and smaller sharks. Occasionally, Jaws appears on the map in the form of the iconic dorsal fin breaking the water's surface.

If players collide with Jaws' dorsal fin, they are able to momentarily control their boat in the side-view encounter and attempt to attack the shark with depth charges. Jaws always collide with the boat, releasing the diver into the water. The shark also appears for a brief moment if a player snags something in the overheard map with Jaws nearby.

One of the most obvious references to Revenge is allowing players to acquire a yellow submersible, with players given three chances to hit the shark and force it to surface and eventually be defeated.

In order to complete the game, the player must jab Jaws with the boat's bow at the proper distance (a la Ellen Brody) when it breaches from the strobe device.

Jaws was featured in the Ultimate Nintendo Guide to the NES Library (1985–1995) by Pat Contri, who posted the following review,

"I remember enjoying this title as a child, but I don't remember playing it much after beating it.

"It wasn't until years later when I remember watching the actual Jaws movie, and being horrified when Quint gets bitten in half in the boat. It was quite a different experience than spearing innocent jellyfish creatures en masse."

Bill Kunkel provided a favourable review of Jaws in the August 1988 issue of Computer Gaming World.

"Jaws is a creative multi-phase action-adventure on which the player battles Universal Pictures' giant shark and a whole cornucopia of his minions," he said.

"Jaws is rich in the small details that make a game playable over long periods of time. Take my word for it, you do not want to confront Big Bruce in the shallows!

"The graphics, animations and gameplay in Jaws are all first-rate. If this is any indication of what LJN can produce in the videogame theatre, they should forget about the wrestling dolls and buck down to full-time game design immediately."

Retro Gamer magazine ran a double-page retrospective of Jaws for their 54th issue, with the reviewer lambasting developers LJN for creating a game more attuned to the plot of Jaws: The Revenge than the original film. He compared the game to the Back to the Future adaptation they had previously released, which had more in common with the game Paperboy, than the film starring Michael J. Fox.

Brett Alan Weiss also reviewed Jaws for allgame.com in 2014 saying,

"In 1975, Steven Spielberg terrified filmgoers with Jaws, a scary movie about a killer shark. In 1987, the folks at Enteractive, Inc bored gamers with Jaws, a non-scary video game about a killer shark.

"The game begins with a dull overhead view of you sailing your boat, trying to avoid the Great White. If Jaws or another sea creature rams your boat, the action switches to a repetitive side-view sequence where you fight as a diver, from a mini-sub or from your boat.

"The goal is to collect enough conch shells (which increase the effectiveness of your attacks) to eventually defeat the shark. But by the time you reach the final anti-climactic scene, you'll be so tired that you won't care if you kill Jaws or not. You'll just be glad the game's almost over."

Below is an exclusive interview with video game artist Ryuichi Nishizawa, who worked on Jaws for Atlus –

Ryuichi Nishizawa – Artist for Jaws NES Game

How did you get involved in working on the Jaws NES video game?

"JAWS" was a contract development project introduced by Atlas Co., Ltd., which we were friends with at that time. We were in charge of everything from planning to delivery of the finished product.

This was quite a rare occurrence at the time, given you mainly produced SEGA games, what was the main factor for developing this game?

Yes, until then our company was only developing arcade games. But we were also interested in console games. We wanted to try NES game development.

What sort of guidelines were you given in terms of the narrative of the game?

Regarding the project, I don't think there was any particular order from the ordering party. I was free to do it.

The game was released shortly after Jaws: The Revenge and also resembles the plot with its narrative, was this coincidence or by design?

Of course, I designed it with the story of the movie in mind. I'm a big fan of Spielberg. I watch all his works. Jaws: The Revenge is not his directorial work, but the great character Jaws was created by him and was planned with respect.

How many developers did it take to work on the game?

Nishizawa, Ishizuka, and Sakamoto. We made it in a fairly short period of time.

Were there any games you had already developed that you used tropes from when developing Jaws?

I think it is influenced by Taito's Polaris and Dragon Quest.

Was there ever any talk of doing a follow-up game?

I don't know.

Did you ever see Jaws: The Revenge, and if so what were your thoughts on it?

I didn't have a chance to see it at that time, but now I can see it on SNS and Youtube. I drew all the pixel art, but it's embarrassing to see it now.

The game has become quite the collector's item for Jaws fans today, are you pleased it is still talked about today?

I didn't know that it was a hot topic. When I think about it now, it's strange that no one objected to expressing that great movie on a game console with low specs at the time.

Jaws The Worst
by B. Harrison Smith

This chapter article. It is not a news release. It is not anything close to resembling legitimate journalism. It is a "fuck you."

The "release" is for Jaws: The Revenge, hitting Variety around the end of 1986. The proposed working title should tell you everything you need to know.

Those familiar with me, my films and my Cynema podcast know that Jaws: The Revenge is my forever thorn in the side. It's my Newman to my Jerry. I call it the worst film ever made, but that's inaccurate because Jaws: The Revenge is not a film.

It's a tax write off and a paycheck. Nothing more.

All you need to do is listen to Episode 2: Jaws the Worst of my Cynema podcast. The film is indefensible and I don't want to repeat a lot of what I have to say there.

To understand the genesis of this mess, you need to go all the way back to 1978 and the set of Jaws 2.

The original Jaws was never intended to have a sequel. Spielberg himself said any sequel would be a "cheap carnival trick." Box office said otherwise and a sequel was demanded by Universal president, Sidney Sheinberg who just happened to be married to Lorraine Gary who just happened to play Chief Brody's wife, Ellen.

Jaws 2's production was plagued with problems. The original director, John Hancock, was fired six weeks into the production. Some say it was because he had too dark of a vision for the film. Others say he was out of his depth and couldn't handle the demands of a big scale action film.

Then there are some who say it was because Hancock refused to bow to Sheinberg's demands for his wife to accompany Brody out to sea and face the final confrontation with the shark with her husband. It is rumoured when producer Daryl Zanuck was told of Sheinberg's intentions to have the script rewritten for Ellen Brody to be part of the climactic ending, he replied "Over my dead body!"

Hancock sided with his producer and Sheinberg struck back. He couldn't fire Zanuck although both men had no love for each other. Zanuck was partnered with David Brown and both were one of the main reasons for the first film's success.

Instead of further jeopardizing the film by firing its producers and director, Hancock was thrown to the shark. He was replaced by TV director Jeannot Szwarc who made the film the studio wanted. Mrs Brody got to go out to sea but never did get to face down the shark with Martin.

By 1986 Sheinberg was on his way out the door to semi-retirement. His wife had already 'retired'. However, Jaws 3-D made a lot of money. Maybe not as much money as the first film, but it was the number one 3-D film for a while and making money even as it was yanked from theatrical release at the end of the summer of 1983 against a tidal wave of bad reviews and word of mouth.

Universal Studios pulled what is known in the business as a 'hit and run'. The film was released as close to the end of the summer season as possible. It would get a strong opening weekend and maybe a few more. By the time bad word of mouth spread, the film recouped and then yanked out of circulation and was taken to cable and home video.

The 'Hit and Run' strategy would apply to the fourth Jaws film. Someone at the studio found there was some extra Jaws money still in the budget lying around.

Allegedly, Sheinberg felt this could be a nice exit payday. Throw together a shit film, everyone gets a check, slap Jaws over the title and who cares if it makes money or not? Everyone would get something out of Los Angeles for the winter with a nice three-month vacation in The Bahamas.

The 'script' which is referenced in the opening Variety article was supposedly 'written' by Sheinberg. However, knowing it was total garbage allowed Michael De Guzman to take full screenwriting credit—or, be left to hold the bag of shit.

Sheinberg made sure to let everyone know...this time his wife was going to get her turn at the bat to slay the shark. There would be no question. The real revenge here is on Richard Zanuck. Sheinberg would get the last laugh which is fitting because this whole 'film' was a joke—on the industry and unfortunately the ticket-buying audience.

Jaws 3-D is a bad film but I don't believe it was intended to be. I think most of the people affiliated with the venture had the best of intentions to make something good. That included director Joe Alves, the remarkable production designer of the first two films.

Alves is on record lamenting over the film being shopped out to schlockmeister Alan Landsburg and unfinished visual effects making it to the screen because budgets and timeframes were cut. The choice of a 3-D entry was a gimmick to cash in on the brief resurrection of the format and it added little to the enjoyment or few thrills of the film.

An original story by Richard Matheson somehow turned into a Sea World misadventure with the Brody brothers and some annoying as hell dolphins. The troubles onset were many, a good cast was wasted and a bad script got made.

However, it takes tremendous effort to make a bad movie. Many don't realize just how hard it is, and the amount of energy misused to do it.

It takes almost no effort to make a cynical one, and this is why Michael Caine's now infamous quote sums up everything about Jaws: The Revenge;

"I have not seen the film, although I hear it is terrible. However, the house it built is terrific."

The abject cynicism of this quote defines everything wrong with not just *Revenge* but the industry as a whole. I got mine and fuck all of you.

The mechanical sharks were shipped to The Bahamas months before there was a script. A story just didn't matter with this. You can almost hear Sheinberg: "Who cares about a story. It's fucking Jaws. Look how they showed up for that last shitty film. This is easy money!"

Picture him chomping on a cigar with stacks of bills and coins on his resolute Black Tower desk and laughing as another bag is dumped out before him.

I was working at Universal around the time the fake sharks were being packed up. I watched fibreglass shark heads and fins lined up for packing. I would walk by the giant tank with a backdrop bigger than a drive-in screen that would serve for the big ending. When a fellow employee told me about the tank for Jaws IV, the "uh oh" factor kicked in right there.

I remember reading that Spielberg chose Cape Cod to get as far away from the Universal executives who wanted him to shoot the ocean scenes on the cheap in their big studio tanks. Spielberg felt it would make it a cheese movie and rightly chose to do what he did which gave us the great film we got.

Instead, director Joe Sargent followed orders and confirmed the climax on the ocean would be shot on the lot.

There was no "directing" going on here. This was a paycheck gun for hire job. They needed someone, and Sargent worked with Lorraine Gary before on a Kojack project called The Marcus Nelson Murders. I bet his name came up, Sheinberg said, yeah get that fuckin' guy. He'll do. He won't have any ideas and will do what needs to be done to crank this turd out.

How Sargent avoided WINNING the Razzie Award for Worst Director is beyond me. He was rightly nominated but was robbed of the award.

You can argue all you want against my theory and my podcast episode. In response, I offer a simple question: "Tell me the plot with a straight face and tell me that you would give almost 25 million to make it."

If you are serious in an answer to the affirmative, I would normally say stay away from filmmaking. In light of some of the trash being greenlit these days, there just might be a place for you in Hollywood.

Imagine walking into the head of Universal Studios and pitching to its president and the board:

"Okay, the shark is psychic..."

If I were the president, I would pull a Donald Trump and before the next sentence could get out, "You're fired," would close the entire pitch session.

Of course, this wasn't pitched. Sheinberg himself admits in that article that opened this piece that HE wrote this shit. He just didn't want to take official screen credit. Nowhere in any of the film's titles is a credit given to Sid Sheinberg for an original story or any story whatsoever. He didn't want that. He hung Michael De Guzman out there to take the 'credit.'

De Guzman is the equivalent of the kid who gets caught by the neighbour after the kid who planned to light a bag of dogshit on the porch runs faster and gets away.

There was no intention to make anything good here. There were no noble efforts. There was no desire to honour the legacy of the original film. This was a fleecing of the budget—a way to milk the last money out of the coffers legally.

Did you ever see the episode of The Office where Steve Carell's Michael Scott is presented with a budget overage from Oscar the accountant? Oscar tells Michael they have to spend this overage or corporate will deduct it from next year's budget.

This is similar to Jaws: The Revenge.

While there were crew who gave their best, this entire production was an insult to art and the hard work expended. The shark didn't have to look good. The script didn't have to be good. The direction just needed to be enough to get them from beginning to end.

Michael Caine actually missed attending the Oscars that year to pick up his statue for Hannah and Her Sisters because he was earning the paycheck that would build his terrific house.

Everything has a price, Michael.

Perhaps the most cynical aspect of this film was the intent to squeeze in as many original movie characters as possible. Sean Brody's death at the opening of the film was meant for Roy Scheider's Chief Brody. Scheider was offered a nice paycheck for likely one day's worth of work to simply telegraph to the audience: "Look Chief Brody is back!"

But wait, Richard Dreyfuss was purportedly hit up to reprise Matt Hooper in a one-day cameo on the phone, calling Michael in The Bahamas. The original script had both parts and can be found online.

This is a cynical ploy to dupe the audience into thinking they just might be getting something good. It might not be Jaws but it could be closer to Jaws 2 and it was definitely not going to be Jaws 3.

It was worse. Far worse.

Jaws 2 was a serviceable sequel. It was made with the highest of production values, sported a great cast and the script by Carl Gottleig did the job. The film's worst crime is that it was not Jaws. But nothing could be.

Like or dislike Jaws 2, it was created to entertain and Zanuck and Brown returned to produce to ensure it would be a good film.

Jaws: The Revenge had none of this and could not blame a green director or farming the film out to a lesser production company like Jaws 3.

No, this had all the ability to be good. The decision was made to simply not do that.

My Cynema podcast is about demanding better of our entertainment. It asks film lovers, entertainment lovers, to research and understands film history...to KNOW what we are consuming because once everything becomes fast food, we have lost our ability to appreciate cuisine.

Jaws: The Revenge is the lowest of shit food at the worst fast food venue in the worst location you can think of.

It is not a film. It is not "so bad it's good."

Jaws the Revenge is just bad.

At the end of the film, the shark ROARS. It literally leaps from the water, roaring out loud with a bad, cheap old special effect from Universal's 1950s monster movie days. The sound was used for Spot, the dragon thing beneath the steps of Herman Munster's home in The Munster's. It was also used as the roar of a giant Praying Mantis in the 1950s big bug movie, The Deadly Mantis.

Much like their insect counterparts, sharks do not have vocal cords or lungs. They couldn't roar if they wanted. Worse yet, the ending credits to *Revenge* boast a scientist and shark expert as part of the crew.

I guess this little fact of nature eluded this "expert."

There was no serious effort to get anything right about this shit show. It was to get a paycheck and if it made money, great. If it didn't, oh well, what's 23 million?

Demand better, folks.

The world around us is not just embracing mediocrity, it's rewarding it.

Jaws: The Revenge is shit, but the money it made is terrific.

Shark Movies Post-Revenge

Jaws: The Revenge may have the dubious honour of killing off the Jaws franchise, but it did not prevent other filmmakers from creating shark thrillers with varying success.

Here we will look at some of the best and worst shark movies that preceded the fourth Jaws film.

Cruel Jaws (1995)

Italian filmmaker Bruno Mattei attempted to piggyback on the name of the Jaws franchise in 1995 with the direct-to-video thriller Cruel Jaws, with a tale of a large shark terrorising a small community in Florida (sound familiar?).

Aatank (1996)

Bollywood was the next filmmaking institute to try and replicate the success of Jaws, with the release of Aatank aka Terror. People living in a coastal village discover black pearls in the ocean but they also disturb a man-eating shark and chaos ensues.

Shark Attack (1999)

Despite being a TV movie, Shark Attack, directed by Bob Misiorowski, boasted recognisable names in Casper Van Dien (Starship Troopers) and Ernie Hudson (Ghostbusters).

When a series of brutal shark attacks disrupt a once serene African fishing village, a marine biologist goes searching for answers.

In what would become a staple of the sub-genre, Shark Attack employed plenty of stock footage of great white sharks and little footage of practical effects or CGI sharks attacking anyone.

Deep Blue Sea (1999)

Shark movies made a comeback to the big screen 12 years after Jaws: The Revenge, with Renny Harlin's Deep Blue Sea. Starring Samuel L. Jackson, Thomas Jane and LL Cool J, a group of scientists at an ocean-based facility attempt to find a cure for Alzheimer's by experimenting on sharks; with disastrous results.

Released in the post-Jurassic Park era, Deep Blue Sea utilised practical effects alongside some computer-generated effects. Interestingly, the film chose to use Mako Sharks, who were enhanced due to their drug injections over the standard great white shark.

Shark Attack 2 (2000)

The mutant sharks introduced in Shark Attack return to wreak more havoc in Cape Town, South Africa with plenty of stock great white shark visuals to pad out the wafer-thin plot.

Shark Attack 3: Megalodon (2002)

The Shark Attack 'franchise' was finally laid to rest three years after beginning, as two Mexican researchers unearth the titular Megalodon and the carnage begins. Notorious for starring a young John Barrowman, who has one notorious line that is worth searching for on YouTube.

Open Water (2003)

Capitalising on the success of The Blair Witch Project, Open Water is based on the experiences of two scuba divers who become stranded in shark-infested waters. On a budget of just $500,000, Open Water would prove a smash hit, grossing $54.6 million worldwide.

Adrift aka Open Water 2: Adrift (2006)

Aiming to capitalise on the success of Open Water, Hans Horn's Adrift was swiftly repackaged as Open Water 2: Adrift for some markets. A group of friends fail to get back on their boat and struggle to survive in the surrounding waters.

The Reef (2010)

Andrew Traucki, who had previous success with the croc thriller Black Water, created arguably the finest non-Jaws shark film with The Reef in 2010. An exercise in tension, a group of friends are hunted by a great white shark after their sailboat capsizes. Traucki manages to blend footage of real sharks with his actors and creates a largely seamless nerve shredder. As of writing, a sequel, The Reef: Stalked, is currently in post-production.

Shark Night 3D (2011)

Jumping on the 3D craze of the 2010s, Shark Night 3D follows a group of seven vacationers who are attacked by sharks while staying at a lake house.

Bait (2012)

A freak tsunami traps shoppers in an Australian town's supermarket with a school of great white sharks. While the CGI sharks have not aged well, Bait is a largely entertaining thriller with some commendable tension sequences.

Sharknado (2013)

Despite starting as a social media joke, Anthony Ferrante's Sharknado gained notoriety after debuting on SyFy in 2013; spawning five sequels to date.

Sharknado reveled in its absurdity, with its over the top performances coupled with the fantastical CGI set pieces inadvertently creating a trash classic by pure accident. The Sharknado franchise has spawned five sequels to date, with 2018's The Last Sharknado: It's About Time the final sequel for now…

The Shallows (2016)

The Sharknado movies may have made a more tongue-in-cheek mockery of the shark thriller but things got serious with Jaume Collet-Serra's The Shallows. After Nancy suffers a shark attack in a secluded Brazilian location, she must plot her escape whilst combating a very angry fish.

The production value behind The Shallows helps it stand above most shark attack thrillers, with a singular plot strand, beautiful cinematography with some of the most realistic CGI shark action seen to date.

47 Metres Down (2017)

After the financial success of The Shallows, Johannes Roberts' shark thriller 47 Metres Down was bumped from a direct-to-video release to a cinematic one. Two sisters vacationing in Mexico go cage diving in shark-infested waters and become stranded at the bottom of the ocean following a freak storm.

47 Metre Down is an exercise in tension with our resident sharks just being the main hindrance to the escape of our two main protag-

onists. Roberts balances his shark action with the human interest narrative that blends perfectly for a taut thriller.

Cage Dive aka Open Water 3: Cage Dive (2017)

Cage Dive was another attempt to revive the Open Water brand, with a group of friends filming a reality show in shark-infested waters. Their footage becomes a diary of death when they start getting picked off by a rogue shark.

Deep Blue Sea 2 (2018)

The glut of moderately successful shark films revived the Deep Blue Sea brand, 19 years after the original release with Deep Blue Sea 2 being produced by SyFy.

The plot involves a billionaire creating five genetically enhanced bull sharks and they wreak havoc on the ocean research facility they are being kept at. Think Deep Blue Sea but with a much lower budget and weaker script.

The Meg (2018)

The big-screen adaptation of Steve Alten's best-selling novel finally made its big-screen debut in 2018, after sitting in development hell for over a decade. Starring Jason Statham, The Meg tells the story of a prehistoric Megalodon that escapes from the Mariana trench and goes on a rampage.

While The Meg did not stick to its source material that closely, it was a joint American and Chinese production that yielded big box office dollars, with filming taking place in New Zealand and China.

A worldwide gross of over $500 million guaranteed a sequel, set for release in 2023, directed by Ben Wheatley.

47 Metres Down: Uncaged (2019)

The first 47 Metres Down film grossed over $62 million at the worldwide box office off a $5 million budget so a sequel was almost guaranteed. Director Johannes Roberts returned for this tale of sisters trapped in an underwater city and hunted by a group of extraordinary sharks. Think The Descent with sharks, but not as well executed.

Great White (2021)

Five plane passengers become stranded at sea when a freak accident sinks their plane plus they have the small matter of man-eating sharks to deal with. A decent enough shark thriller that is let down by some pretty shoddy CGI great whites, unfortunately.

Interviews

Lorraine Gary (Ellen Brody)

Can you recall your reaction to your late husband Sid pitching Jaws '87 to you?

I've no clear memories of Sid telling me. I guess I was excited. A bit nervous since I'd left that world and was working pro bono for foster children as well as having completed three years as a literary agent.

You had stepped away from the acting game at this point, was there any apprehension about coming back?

I'd never lost my love of acting but I'd aged out.

But life was family and dabbling in agenting and trying to produce films. Someday I'll talk about that.

This was a fast turnaround from script to production, how did it feel to be back in Edgartown filming a Jaws movie?

Can you recall what your initial discussions were like with Joseph Sargent?

Talking with Joe was easy. He and his wife were our friends. We had worked together before in the Marcus Nelson murders which was the pilot for Kojack…. Telly Savalas. I thought Joe was a lovely man but a bit intimidated by following Steven (Spielberg). But Joe trusted me.

Did you have any thoughts about where Ellen Brody would be at this point in her life?

I never think of where she'd be. Probably like me…. Widowed, grieving but living. Family son and his gang. Back in Amity and reading/streaming to fill the loneliness. Maybe still selling real estate.

You have excellent on-screen chemistry with on-screen sons Mitchell Anderson and Lance Guest, how did you approach those scenes?

I got to know Lance a bit and liked him very much. I am at heart a mother.

Michael Caine has spoken warmly about working with you, what was Michael like on-set?

I was terrified to work with Michael. I knew him socially a bit and respected him enormously as an actor. The night before our first table reading I was crazy scared. I took a sleeping pill and woke with remnants of chocolate chip cookies all over me.
    I blamed our dog.
    Then I saw myself as I brushed my teeth.
    I'm eating out of fear….. unconscious out of fear.
    Michael was so professional and kind. I heard great music from his trailer. I asked and he had flown to New York and saw Phantom of the Opera and bought the disc.
    Michael was allowed a weekend away. I was not and very jealous. After one of his trips, he surprised me and gave me a cd/or tape of the score. I was thrilled and grateful. It's haunting and lovely.
    At one time when we were miked in a car, I started chatting and he stopped me. Not professional. He was right.

Did you think it was a bold choice to have a middle-aged romance as a main part of the narrative?

"Bold choice" of middle age romance is crap. You are not dead romantically at 50. It really was more of a flirtation based on loneliness. There was no feeling of a formal relationship.

Were you surprised to get the call to go back in for the reshot ending where Jake survived? Also, did the tank water at Universal dye your hair?

I have no memory of getting called to shoot Jake's survival. And no… my hair was coloured blonde and the chemicals in the pool …. Any pool…. Cause colour damage. No big deal.

I found it harsh that you carried the burden of the criticism of the film. Did this put you off staying in Hollywood in a producer or acting capacity?

The only criticism I remember is of the shoulder pads in my wardrobe. I thought they looked cool. No other criticism flowed down to me.

I played a grieving woman in a strange and unknown community.

Did you ever rewatch the film and if so what did you think of it?

I never watch the movie. It was third rate and I have no desire to see myself.

My kids and grandkids enjoy it. So that was good that came from it.

Lance Guest (Michael Brody)

As far as I am aware, you didn't audition for the role, is that correct?

They just called me and offered me the role. They called my agent in like November (1986) and we started shooting at the end of January.

Is that sort of practice unheard for someone who had been working regularly for a few years?

In my case, you get to sort of point where you are offered stuff and don't have to audition but I wasn't really there yet. I had done The Last Starfighter, and a lot of people liked that movie but it wasn't considered a hit, so I wasn't on anybody's A-list. That movie didn't make any money and I had continued to audition for other things.

I had been working in TV a lot at this point, I had done The Last Starfighter and Halloween II, I had just done two plays that previous summer, and they called and said I'd been offered Jaws '87. I am old enough to remember Johnny Carson used to make jokes about sequels, they don't have the same cache as they have now. Other than The Godfather Part II, sequels didn't get a lot of love.

The original Jaws was one of the greatest movies of all time, which I still watch every time it comes on. It's like a perfect movie to me.

What was the Jaws brand seen as at this point in time going into pre-production?

I was pretty hard on movies and thought everything was a sell-out, and probably unfairly. It was called Jaws '87, which just reminded me of Airport 75, and I don't think there were necessarily high hopes for it. I think I was contracted to Universal for three films after The Last Starfighter, so I don't know if that was part of me getting the role.

The reason I got the call was because the director Joe Sargent had seen me audition for a film he directed about a group of nuns who were killed in El Salvador in the early 80s. Joe had seen and I didn't get the part, Peter Barton got the part.

Joe said to me, 'Y'know why I called you in?', it was because of the movie about the nuns and you were really good (auditioning).

I read the script and it was a fine script, it definitely had a different point of view, it was from the mom's point of view. It was more of a family orientated story, she's like a momma grizzly with her kids. She's very protective of her children, which was apparent from the first film, so it was decided to go with that narrative.

I read and thought, this isn't bad, it's not cheesy, it's slightly unbelievable with the group of sharks that seem to have it out for the Brody's. It kind of had the same vibe as Jason from the Friday the 13th movies vibe, he keeps coming back to life and we had the same sharks attacking the same family. All of this was apparent in the first one, as that was about an island that had a shark problem, but when you start sequelising it you want to make a continuum. There have been common elements, such as the shark, and the family, you can't just set it somewhere else.

It is so hard to duplicate the things that made Jaws so special.

Michael's (De Guzman) script weaved the believability into the story, the same as the most outlandish horror films. Upon first reading, it was like, okay I'd buy it. I had to basically track my character's behaviour through the events and it wasn't that bad with the original script.

Three days before we started shooting, we got another script and all the scenes had been switched around because they basically found that the stunts that were written into the script for the animatronic shark, only some of them could actually happen. Because the whole thing was thrown together quickly, they only got confirmation from the special effects about what could and could not be done in a short time frame.

Even though this was post-Last Starfighter, CGI was not the practice.

What were some of the things that were in that original script which didn't happen?

It was explained to me, the balance of the events, and motivations were scrambled at the last minute to accommodate the effects they could actually do. This was how it was explained to me, and I was like freaking out, and Joe had to talk me off the ledge.

What was it like filming in Edgartown?

I remember Sid Sheinberg, and everyone was passing around Mako Shark sushi, and Sid said to me, 'Me and the sharks have an agreement, I don't eat them, they don't eat me'. That was during a cast party in Edgartown. It was fun. We were there at the end of January and we had four feet of snow and it was very interesting. It's typically more of a summer place not a winter place, but it was fun for me.

You have such a contrast because after a few days in Martha's Vineyard you jet off to Nassau. Isn't the climate quite volatile there?

It is the Bermuda Triangle, or thereabouts. That was the other thing whilst shooting, and I got reasons why we couldn't get certain things, but we would sometimes go out to shoot and sometimes be out all day long waiting for the water to calm down because if the water was in any way rough it wouldn't match any of the stuff we'd previously shot. The film crew would only shoot when the lighting and the sun was right, when the water was right, none of that stuff you can really fake.

We did a lot of stuff in the Universal tank at the end, because it was also cloudy in California.

A lot of the underwater scenes that we used scuba gear for, were often churned up by the weather and the tides, as you can't see when the conditions are like that. We thought we were gonna get that picturesque Bahamas-look, but we only got that some of the time because it was Springtime in the Bermuda Triangle.

One of my favourite scenes is the chase through the shipwreck, how much of that was filmed by you?

The stunt guy's name was Gavin (McKinney), he did most of the swimming and I did all of the closeups. I did a few things, like swimming into the Bond wreck, as it had previously been used on a Bond film. I swam around a corner and turned to look at him (the shark), and it was kind of a cool move. A lot of the time it was Gavin's hands as he has more freckles than me, but I was on what they called topside most of the time, so on my days off I would go on second unit and get closeups.

You didn't have many days off then?

No, even on the days off we still had to be there. We would go out on the boats and wait for the skies to be right and if they didn't we have to go back to shore.

In terms of the family dynamic, it works well on-screen, so were there any screen tests done between you, Lorraine, Karen Young and Judith Barsi?

No, we were just cast. We did do some read throughs for like three days and I was really glad to have done that because then you kind of know how you are going to do it. I was used to read throughs from working in theatre and you get a sense of the rhythm, although this was with the old script, and on our final read-through we got a brand new script right before we started shooting. I just thought any credibility this had would just be shot.

The Editor (Michael Brown) said something nice to me, as he said he'd cut to me to help keep the story on track. That's one of the greatest compliments you can give an actor.

Regarding the shark, there were nine models, how temperamental were they to work with?

Definitely as it was all hydraulics, which were all done on these X frames that were put on the bottom of the Caribbean sea. It was like 40, maybe 20 feet deep in parts we were filming, so it wasn't that deep. Anything would affect it, the tides, it was very, very difficult. They historically didn't have a lot of prep time, so they did the best they could with what they had and halfway through the shoot I was like, 'next time fake people, real sharks'.

You think the film is completed around May, you get a call from Sid in June to come back in, what can you tell us about that?

It was Joe who actually called me, and said 'come down to the beach', and we'll film down there. This was when Joe was living in Malibu, and I was like sure I'll film down there.

Mine and Joe's birthdays are like a day apart, and it was around that time, so I said by the way happy birthday Joe.

He said Mario tested so well that they didn't want him to die, which was the reason for the reshoot.

So instead of Malibu, you end up at the Universal backlot, how long did that take to complete?

There weren't that many stunts, it was mainly about just shooting the ending. We were in that tank in June, which was not the best time if you wanted sun. The biggest problem effects-wise was getting the ending. They did everything they could to run the shark into bowsprit, but then it ended up exploding, I don't know what happens (laughs).

Michael De Guzman was on-set, was he rewriting as you filmed?

Yeah he was there. Michael's a good writer, he would use a typewriter and carry that around with him. He was an old school guy, always had his Boston Red Sox hat on, with a New England accent.

There is one scene I have to ask you about, the angry welder scene. Was that line in the script or improvised?

I thought that line was hilarious, and I laughed out loud when I read that line. Other people didn't find it as funny but I did.

Did you attend a premiere for filming ahead of its release?

The movie was released and then they decided about changing the ending for the European release. I did go to a premiere and it was just at Universal Studios and brought the family down and the girl I was dating at the time. I don't remember we made too big a deal about it.

You've got a scene between you, Michael and Mario near the end of the film in the plane, what were your experiences sharing scenes with them?

I've told this story a million times, but Michael Caine saved my life. Mario and I were in the tiny speedboat and at the time I weighed about 160 pounds, and it was me, John McPherson the DP and a big ass camera. Were in the back with the motor and Mario, 200 pounds of solid muscle, he was up in front and we shot. We shot his angle and then we turned around on me, so it's Mario, the camera and John against me and the boat motor on the other end.

The battery pack for the camera is at the bottom of the boat and covered in plastic so it doesn't short out when it gets wet. It's still submerged in water and it has a considerable amount of voltage.

The whole boat goes down and floods, that battery pack gets covered with water, I feel this hand and the barge is like three or four feet away from us, and Michael Caine is doing the off-camera dialogue. As soon as that goes under, the cameraman throws the $250,000 camera onto the barge so that it doesn't go down, he bails out and I feel this hand grab my shirt, Michael Caine 'get the fuck out of that boat!', he pulls me out and I was like whoa!

I said to Michael you've just saved my life, he just said, 'ah you don't know about those things.'

The funny thing was I only weighed 160 pounds so he could do it with one hand.

And what about working with Mario?

Mario, he's a pretty funny guy.

When we were filming at the universal tank, we were on lunch and the studio tour tram went by and the tourists would stare at us sitting around eating lunch (fun, huh?) he just jumped up and said 'let's go jump on the back of the tram and ride it till the end' which we did, much to the surprise of the guide, who was forced to go off-script 'Well… it's looks like we are being , um…. joined by a couple of…. Um the , um…. Actors here, they are working … as I said, on the new ….Jaws movie…(etc.)'

We were soaking wet in our wetsuits just dripping all over the tram enjoying the Guide's complete confusion. Then we got off and returned to the set. Mario was THAT kind of guy. He knew it would be fun for the tourists, which hopefully it was.

Some of your scenes with Lorraine are the family drama element of the story, tell us about working with her?

The impression I got was that she had been looking after her family since Jaws 2, and she hadn't been working that much as an actress. Being thrust back into the lead role in this movie she was very overly conscious of herself. She's a very naturalistic actress, in the rehearsals she was very real and low key. She didn't need to be overly conscious because she was great and had a real handle on it.

She and I got on really well, and I was really fond of her.

Was Sid Sheinberg on-set much?

I remember him being there a few times because it was kind of his thing. He was the driving force for a new Jaws film. He would come and see Lorraine and see the crew, but he didn't say very much.

Your on-screen brother is Mitchell Anderson, did you two actually get to meet when filming as you don't physically share a scene?

Yeah, I think so. He was there when we first got to Martha's Vineyard and I knew him from something else. I think I did a TV show with him, some sort of afterschool special.

Have you ever heard about the novelisation of Jaws: The Revenge?

I have a copy but I didn't read it.

There is a voodoo priest in it, that's after you…

Oh really, cool.

Michael Caine's character is also an undercover CIA agent on a drug bust

Well that was an idea from the original script, the reason Michael Brody was so mistrustful of Hoagie was that he saw him dealing with drug dealers. It wasn't real but the audience was supposed to think it was, and then it was downplayed in the script.

When the film was released it was probably one of the last practical effects animal attack movies, was there ever a discussion of continuing the series beyond *Revenge*?

I think if they ever did make another Jaws movie they'd have to use CGI. The animatronics did cripple parts of the production as you don't ever have full control over them. You've seen those Marvel movies, they do crazy stuff.

There is a scene in the script, where Michael speaks to Matt Hooper on the telephone. Do you think the studio was confident of getting Richard Dreyfuss for a cameo?

I think they left that in the script as long as they could and hoped Richard Dreyfuss wanted to come back. They never made the deal so it didn't happen.

Requels have become popular again in horror right now with Scream (2022) et al. If the call came in to do another Jaws, would you consider it?

I don't know if I see that happening…sure.

Mitchell Anderson (Sean Brody)

How did you get the part in Jaws: The Revenge?

I auditioned for the role with the director Joe Sargent. It was one of the rare instances, especially that early in my career, when there was not a long audition process. I believe I got the part based on just two auditions.

What was it like working with Lorraine Gary?

She was lovely. I really only worked with her for a couple of weeks. Much of my time on the movie was spent alone in a big tank on the Universal lot. The exteriors were shot on location in Martha's Vineyard for two weeks. So Lorraine and I spent quite a bit of time together, which helped with our short, but important on screen relationship.

The film itself has become a cult phenomenon over the years, do you ever get questions about it?

All the time. It seems to air a lot on tv. Whenever it's on I get text messages and emails from friends and family all over the country. It's funny how ten minutes in a film like Jaws, The Revenge can leave such a lasting legacy. The best is when the children of friends and family see it for the first time, the new generation, they get a kick out of the idea that I was in it. And that I get killed in such a brutal way!

Your death scene is one of the most graphic in the entire series, tell us about filming that?

We did most of the exterior long shots in January in Martha's Vineyard. It was cold! I think it took three or four nights in the harbor to get all the shots. While I had a stuntman for the last moment, getting pulled under, the rest of it was me. The special effects people worked hard to make it as graphic as possible. They rigged a blood tube and pump around my back and out my sleeve where the shark chomped my arm. The night we did that close up, it was about 20 degrees, it was about 3am, and I remember freezing my ass off! It took an hour in a hot shower to wash off all the blood and get warm. I do think that one shot, when Sean realizes his arm is gone, is pretty real. Even now, when I see it, it gives me chills. And as a note – my mother was not having it. She saw the movie, but basically cried for the rest of the film after my death scene. And just when she was back to normal, they did that quick flashback at the end. She still talks about how difficult it was to see that.

The scene itself was one I found quite disturbing at a young age, with the choir singing as you were being eaten, was this always Joe Sargeant's vision?

I think it was disturbing and actually one of the best scenes in the movie. If you're making a thriller, you want it to be SO uncomfortable and scary. It was most definitely Joe's vision to begin the movie this way.

What was your favourite day on set on Revenge?

It was all fun. I was a young actor and this was my first big movie experience. But the day I still talk about is when I was filming in the tank at Universal. They had a replica of the boat on hydraulics in the middle of this huge pool. We were shooting my close up POV shots as the shark attacked the boat and took my arm, finally pulling me under the water. The hydraulics were to shake and roll the boat as it was getting attacked. At one point, I was out there alone on the boat waiting while they set up a shot, and I heard this crash. The boat had fallen off the rack. I called out to the crew on the other side of the pool, "Uh guys? I think I'm sinking." They laughed and said I was just being dramatic. But sure enough, two minutes later, the boat sank to the bottom of the tank and I swam to the side. It was all pretty funny, if you don't count the days lost and the money spent fixing it. It became a story in Army Archard's column in the Hollywood Reporter and is sort of part of the lore of Jaws: The Revenge. At least it's a story I tell all the time when people ask me about the movie.

In an alternate version do you wish it was you who got to go to the Bahamas and fight the shark?

Well sure. Who wouldn't? I would have loved the experience of shooting in the Bahamas and being a bigger part of the movie.

What was your initial reaction when you saw the finished film?

Well, I knew instantly it would achieve cult status. But I also knew it was going to get roundly panned by the press. I think the year it came out it may have gotten a couple of Razzies (for worst movie). For me though, it was only a great experience. I was in a huge studio movie, and even though it wasn't a huge part, I had opening title credits AND an iconic death scene at the hands (or jaws) of the world's most famous shark.

Karen Young – Carla Brody

What was it like filming in the Bahamas?

I remember the film being a fantastic excuse to spend time in the Bahamas, and that during free time, the cast did some snorkeling.

You had a handful of scenes in Edgartown, how much time did you spend there and did you get a chance to sample the local hospitality?

Edgartown was a wintery spell prior to going off to the Bahamas, but as I'd never been there, I enjoyed the picturesque village.

What can you tell us about working with both Michael Caine and Lorraine Gary?

Michael Caine was effervescent as an acting comrade and very funny. Lorraine was simply the sweetest person on the entire set, and we were good friends during the filming and we stayed in touch afterwards whenever I was in Los Angeles.
   Lance Guest and I haven't crossed paths again, sadly.

You worked on some massive projects post-Jaws such as Daylight and the Sopranos, did being in JTR open more doors for you in Hollywood?

I think the film would have opened more doors for me in Hollywood had it made more money than it did (my recollection is that it did poorly).

Today you are a judge for the highly successful Maine International Film Festival with your husband. How did you find the transition from acting to critiquing films?

As for the Maine Int. Film Festival, as my husband is the Programming Director, I agreed to program the shorts as a way to lessen his load, as previously, he had programmed them in addition to the features.

Robert W. Harris – Utility Sound Technician

Tell us how you got involved with Jaws the Revenge?

A good friend was hired as the unit photographer and he told me the film hadn't hired a publicist yet. I'd just finished working on Dragnet for Universal and I guess they liked my work on that, so when I told the director of publicity I was interested in JTR, he submitted my name to the director and producers and I was hired.

You had worked on some massive films such as The Goonies, at this point in your career, how did this compare?

I worked on The Goonies. That was one of my all-time favourites to have worked on, so comparisons wouldn't be fair.

What was the atmosphere like on-set for Revenge?

The mood varied. On Martha's Vineyard, where filming began, there was some excitement about making a Jaws movie where the original had been filmed. But the shark didn't work there. Once we got to the Bahamas and the shark action, it was more fraught, since, like the problems with the original Jaws, the shark either malfunctioned or just didn't look right. There was a lot of trying to figure out ways to shoot around it – some successful, some not.

For those who aren't sure, can you break down what a Utility Sound Technician takes care of on-set?

Utility sound pulls the cable and attaches mikes to actors.

Did you get to work at Martha's Vineyard and the Bahamas?

Yes.

What was the most difficult scene to be part of for you personally?

The boat scenes in the Bahamas were most difficult for the shooting crew and most frustrating for me – especially when we had visiting press – because there usually wasn't room on the main camera boat for non-essential personnel. There was a support boat I took some visitors on a few times but not much you could see from there. Most of us stayed on-shore during the water sequences.

Was it already decided that the shark would roar when filming got underway?

I don't know

Did you or your team have many discussions with Joseph Sargent or the Producers?

Regular conversations with producer/director Joe Sargent, who was lovely, and became good friends with the screenwriter, Michael De Guzman, who was around the whole time.

Can you remember the most difficult day on-set for you?

I rarely remember those.

This was a fast shoot, especially given the size of the production, did it feel like the film was being rushed?

Fast? As I recall, the shoot went way over-schedule and we wound up shooting additional weeks in the tank at Universal.

Was Sidney Sheinberg present on-set any time?

Mr Sheinberg visited his wife for a few days in the Bahamas but I don't recall him being on set much.

Jordan Klein Sr. – Director of Photography (Second Unit)

Tell us how you got involved in Jaws the Revenge?

I got into the Jaws film after the first cameraman wasn't getting the job done.

I take it your work on films & TV such as Flipper, Cocoon, Splash and Jaws 3D made you an obvious choice?

I'm certain, having done many other underwater films was a factor.

What scenes were involved in the second unit of filming?

First of all I designed and built the 3D underwater housing for the Arri that was used. The scenes, all the open ocean scenes at Grand Cayman as well as scenes In the tank in Orlando.

Your crew was involved in the attack scene of Michael Brody in the one-man submersible, tell us how you went about designing this machine?

I have designed and built a number of subs both wet and dry, my first was for Flipper, then many more for films like the bomb carriers for both Thunderball, Never say Never and more.

Sea shoots are notoriously difficult going back to the original Jaws, did you have any problems when filming in the Bahamas?

No, the Bahamas has always treated me well and provided help when they could provide it both with customs and immigration.

What discussions did you have with Joseph Sargent during production?

I was given storyboards for my first day's shoot, after dailies arrived, Joe packed up and went back to the studio in LA and left me in charge to finish. The underwater shots lasted about 10 days.

Jaws the Revenge was a rushed shoot, did you feel any pressure on the scenes you worked on?

No pressure, you get up early, get out to the barge and start the day, panic or rushing doesn't get it done.

How did you find working with the mechanical sharks?

Working with the shark was very difficult. I had no direct communication; a diver stayed behind me with a camera to show the shark operator my hand directions....today underwater sound would have saved 50% of the time per shot.

Do you have any funny stories from on-set?

I'm sure there but I'm having problems recalling this information, sorry.

How did you combine a love for scuba diving and photography?

I've been a water bug since age 5 as I was raised on Miami Beach and spent my time staying wet...designed and made my own fins mask (they weren't being made yet).

How did your work on Jaws 3D differ from working on Revenge?

3D was a very technical shoot, we planned everything but Revenge was a more typical shoot and planning was more, just checking the storyboards jump in and get it.

Donna Honig – Extra, Hair Dresser in Edgartown and Jaws Tours guide

When did you first hear about the crew of Jaws the Revenge coming to Edgartown?

We first heard about it in the first week of January and the crew began setting up towards the end of the month. They were running quite a tight schedule and needed to be in the Bahamas by the 7th of February.

I hear there were open auditions for locals to play extras, did you hear about this?

Yes, there was an article in the Vineyard Gazette with an open casting call for extras and a lot of the townsfolk got involved. They needed people to be in the choir whilst Sean is being attacked plus others for his funeral scene soon after.

Did you get to spend any time around the set, if so what scenes did you see being filmed?

Yes, I was actually in one scene, where Sean is going across the docks towards his boat. I am putting up Christmas decorations next to the dock. Originally I was also going to conduct the choir but they decided to use another person for that.

How much does a production like Jaws the Revenge do for the local economy?

It certainly helps because at that time of year a lot of islanders will decide to vacation in Florida while the weather is colder and there are fewer tourists. The cast and crew when they arrived invited all the town to a party where they got to know people. This was a big boost and helped us all feel part of the film.

You knew the late Lee Fierro, was she part of the open auditions for Jaws the Revenge?

I think Lee knew Janice Hall who was in charge of casting for the Amity sets and had kept in touch over the years since they filmed back in 1974. It was a nice bit of continuity to have Lee involved in scenes with Lorraine to help connect back to the original.

Did you and Lee keep in touch in the years up until her death?

Yes, we saw each other on and off from time to time. I sometimes run private location tours for Jaws in Edgartown so in the past, I would give Lee a call and see if she'd be interested in coming along and talking to people about her experiences in the film. Lee was a big local theatre person and worked a lot with the young children in the area and was always up for talking about Jaws.

Were there any special screenings of the film around its release in local cinemas?

Yes, we had a special screening shortly after the film's release where all the people who got to be extras got to see the film. I must admit I laughed through half of it, as we were all just trying to recognise ourselves in shots and it was a lot of fun. The premiere was at the same venue we had a screening of the original Jaws back in 1975.

Why do you think Edgartown is the perfect location for Amity?

Edgartown is such a close-knit community, which makes it the perfect location to be Amity. Everyone kind of knows everyone around here and looks out for each other. Having two Jaws films come to town was a great boost for the town and it was so much fun to have so many local people involved.

Diana Hamman – Miniature Designer and Painter

Tell us how you got involved in Jaws the Revenge?

I'd worked for Ted Rae a couple of times before. He hired me as a miniature maker and painter on Jaws: The Revenge.

How much did you know about the project before signing on?

I knew and really liked the original Jaws. I never read the script for this movie. This is typical for an FX technician. You're hired as an artist/worker & are only told what you need to know to do the work you're assigned. Back then, if you asked, your boss would usually share the script (or pages of the scene you were working on if that's all they had). I usually asked!

Your main task was designing a miniature of Neptune's Folly. Tell us about the process of putting the model together?

Ted asked me to create "flotsam & jetsam" for the boat –small-scale versions of items on deck that washed overboard in the scene. These items needed to float so I made them out of balsa wood. Some were small-scale copies of items in still photographs from the live-action shots. I also created a few miscellaneous "boat deck items" from scrap balsa wood.

I also did some scenic aging on the miniature boat. Ted taught me to "age-paint" in higher contrast for scenes shot in smoke or water. I always cringe a bit when looking at miniature sets I painted in bright light. But this type of aging works well when you're shooting through "atmosphere".

I take it your scenes were filmed at Universal Studios and you couldn't get in a trip to the Bahamas?

I only worked at Ted Rae's shop in the San Fernando Valley. He shot the FX scenes on his stage there. Ted had two units rented – one was a clean, well-organized shop where we worked & one was his stage.

I wish I'd gone to the Bahamas – love it there! ;)

This was a notoriously rushed shoot; how much pressure was put on you and your team to turn around your work in double quick time?

I don't remember feeling particularly rushed on this shoot. When we worked on Beetlejuice we were really rushed. For me, this was a calm, easy job with fun people, great conversation, and Ted's always-interesting (& occasionally mockable) music choices in the background.

Did you have any discussions with Joseph Sargent or any of the production crew about any particulars they wanted for Neptune's Folly?

I didn't. I took my orders directly from Ted Rae. Ted was the head of his own FX shop/studio. He was the shop foreman, Director of Photography, Editor, and Optical FX artist. He took meetings with producers & directors. I just showed up and tried to do what he told me to do as well as I could. Ted has very high standards and expects his crews to do great work & people deliver because he creates beautifully executed, artistic shots.

What was the harder model to build, the full boat or the broken boat from the finale?

You'd have to ask Tom Gleason who built the miniature boat. Typically, broken things are much harder to make. Imagine all those broken surfaces having to be just right!

Were your miniatures used for the reshot ending with the shark being impaled by the boat?

No idea.

Have you kept in touch with any of the crew from Jaws: The Revenge in the intervening years?

I've kept up with Ted Rae through the years. We're good friends & I continue to admire his work. I'm Facebook friends with Tom

Gleason & I caught up with him a few years ago. I think Marc Tyler worked on it – and we remain lifelong pals.

How did this compare to your work on Gremlins 2 and Night of the Creeps?

Ted Rae was my boss on Night of the Creeps, too – in his earlier studio space (in Van Nuys, I think – next to Jim Danforth's shop). Night of the Creeps had a smaller crew. I think it was only Ted, me, the late, great Tony Rupprecht and Todd Masters (it was Todd's second job in L.A.). The Creeps set was a really fun miniature to make & paint. Also, I had fun shopping for ½ scale items for the set – a few sample sizes were perfectly to scale & saved a lot of time!

Tony & I had a lot of fun goofing around during the stop-mo shoot. We each had only one thing to do per shot. Ted had to take the shot, then run-up to the miniature, move a bunch of Creeps for several minutes, then come back, take the shot, repeat.

With the emergence of computer graphics miniature models are not used as much in movies these days, do you think filmmakers are missing a trick by not using them more in big blockbusters?

Yes. Miniatures still read as more real to my eye. I'd always choose to use miniatures whenever possible & supplement with digital environments when there are budget restrictions. Occasionally, digital scenery makes more sense – but for me, that's rare.

Did you get a chance to see the finished version of Jaws the Revenge?

I must have…but I don't remember. I know I saw the finished footage of the scene I worked on. Life was very busy in those days, moving from job to job. With the long hours, it wasn't possible to see every film I worked on.

The Legacy of Jaws: The Revenge

Bruce Jnr breaches one last time…

When considering the legacy of Jaws: The Revenge, 35 years after its release – the most obvious measure is the fact we have yet to see another Jaws film surface.

Revenge was the final nail in the coffin, it seems, for Universal who washed their hands of the franchise after its domestic box office ($20 million), didn't even break even on the $23 million budget.

For the director Joe Sargent, it seemed a bridge too far, in terms of breaking into big-budget Hollywood blockbusters with him seeing out his directorial career in the same space he had operated in pre-Revenge, the direct-to -TV movies.

For headline star Lorraine Gary, her return to acting firmly hit the buffers, although it is unclear whether she simply returned to the screen on the insistence of husband Sid Sheinberg or if this was set to be a career re-launch of sorts. Gary had, at the time of production of *Revenge*, alluded to wanting to go into producing rather than acting in the future.

Other top-line cast fared better, with Mario Van Peebles really finding his stride as an actor plus a director, most notably with New Jack City, alongside Wesley Snipes. Lance Guest, much the same as director Sargent, returned to television work and continues to work to this day, with rumours of a long gestated sequel to The Last Starfighter always swirling around.

Guest's on-screen wife Karen Young bagged notable roles in the Stallone action feature Daylight (1997) before securing a recurring role on the critically acclaimed HBO series The Sopranos. Today, alongside husband Ken Eisen, she co-ordinates the Maine International Film Festival, judging short films for selection from all over the world.

Despite his absence from the Oscars, Michael Caine also continued to work steadily before his career had a real renaissance in the early 2000s with the gangster feature Shiner, the third Austin Powers movie Goldmember (playing Austin's father Nigel) plus most notably his turn as Alfred in Christopher Nolan's Dark Knight trilogy.

Caine continues to disown the film, but as the infamous quote goes, he cannot deny the house it helped him build for his mother.

Jaws: The Revenge also didn't harm the exploits of Lynn Whitfield, who has worked steadily (mainly in television) up until the present day, starring in shows such as How To Get Away With Murder, Without a Trace and Greenleaf.

In terms of blockbuster scale aquatic horror, *Revenge* would also be the last notable use of practical effects to create monsters on the big screen. Just four years later, James Cameron would release Terminator 2: Judgment Day, using computer-generated effects he had experimented with in The Abyss (1989); and would change cinema forever.

After T2 blew audiences away, one Steven Spielberg latched onto CGI and created the classic Jurassic Park, which blended computer-generated dinosaurs with large scale, animatronic models, in what was seen as a watershed moment that would effectively see the passing of the torch from practical to computer effects. It's kind of ironic that the man who created Jaws, ultimately was probably the one to put the final nail in the coffin of the old school filming methods and animatronic sharks that had become the norm across the four films.

This isn't to say the shark models were without their problems, as you can trace back in this book and other chronicles of the first three Jaws films and you can guarantee that there were points when the mechanical sharks simply wouldn't work.

Having said this, in the intervening years, as we have chronicled in a previous chapter, there has been a slew of imitators to Jaws' aquatic horror crown, mainly featuring computer-generated sharks and other beasts, with the closest we have come to anything close to Spielberg's classic was the CGI shark from 2016's The Shallows, given the attention to detail they employed to get the shark actually moving and behaving like a live animal.

The question still remains; will we see another Jaws movie?

The horror genre is on a crest of nostalgia for past glories with the Halloween franchise enjoying a box office renaissance under the guidance of David Gordon Green and other properties such as Hellraiser and The Exorcist set to be resurrected with significant financial backing over the coming years.

But what does a Jaws movie look like today?

Spielberg has reportedly vetoed efforts to remake the 1975 film, with quotes attributed to Deadline stating that he has been approached about the potential project and has remained firm on his resistance. Could this be due to his traumatic experience filming it or does he simply want one of his masterpieces left alone? Probably a bit of both.

If a remake is out of the question, what would a fast-forward sequel ala Halloween (2018) look like? Could a new generation of Brodies, led by Thea or Michael and Carla return to Amity many years after *Revenge* and run into a whole new shark problem?

Maybe Larry Vaughn Jr. is now the Mayor? The possibilities are endless, given the universe that Jaws created over its four films.

The elephant in the room remains the appetite for it though, as Jaws: The Revenge is still sneered at by the masses and news of a sequel that even remotely references it could do a new film damage before cameras have even rolled.

Would the loyal Jaws enthusiasts from the past, 47 years (at the time of writing) accept a computer-generated Bruce or would NBCUniversal take a punt on using animatronic one more time to placate their established fanbase?

For now though, Jaws: The Revenge remains the final Jaws film, polarising fans of the series to this day, often seen on many people's Christmas watch lists on Letterboxd. I guess the fact we are still talking about this film 35 years later is the best legacy it can have.

The shark is still roaring, and we are still listening.

Paul Downey
May 2022.

Thank You's

I would like to express my extreme gratitude to the following people (in no particular order) who have helped to make The Shark Is Roaring: The Story of Jaws: The Revenge a reality -

Brannon Carty, Bryan Matthew Garner, Steven Bayman, Jonathan Sheinberg, Lorraine Sheinberg, Lance Guest, Mitchell Anderson, Jordan Klein Sr., Diane Hamman, Karen Young, Donna Honig, Ken Eisen, Brendan Haley, David Storey, Shaun O'Rourke, Steve DeJarnett, Padraic Maroney, Ben Ohmart, B. Harrison Smith, Kevin McAfee, Andrew McNess, Ross Williams, Jim Beller, Michael de Guzman, Robin Block, David Wiener, Robert D. Harris, Ryuichi Nishizawa, Celia N. Foster, Sean Kemp, Diane Hyams

Index

1

1987 15, 16, 19, 20, 25–28, 35, 36, 40, 42, 43, 45, 47, 48, 56, 64, 66, 67, 84, 87–89, 91, 95, 96, 136, 154, 156

A

Aatank 166
Aliens 19, 96
Amblin 22, 35
AMC 117, 118, 120, 121
Amity 11, 15, 25, 28, 33, 42–44, 46, 56, 67, 68, 71, 73, 75, 77, 80, 81, 83, 102–6, 108, 116, 124, 138–40, 145, 173, 193, 194
Anderson, Mitchell 26, 28, 32, 45, 65, 75, 103, 173, 182, 184

B

Bahamas 11, 24, 27, 42, 44, 47, 50, 51, 55, 62–64, 69–71, 74, 76–78, 80–83, 85, 89, 92, 106, 110, 115, 118, 124, 125, 129, 130, 134, 136, 137, 140, 147, 153, 160, 162, 164, 186–92, 195
Barbarosa 36
Barrowman, John 167
Barsi, Judith 12, 16, 30–32, 76, 147–53, 178
Batman Returns 39
Beetlejuice 39, 195
Benchley, Peter 26, 47

Brody 25–27, 30–32, 34, 41, 43–46, 49, 51, 52, 56, 58, 59, 64, 67–71, 75, 76, 78–80, 82, 97, 102, 103, 105, 107, 114, 124, 125, 129, 136, 138–42, 144, 155, 159–61, 164, 172, 173, 175, 183, 184, 187, 191

C

Caddyshack 38
Caine, Michael 11, 13, 15, 31, 34, 44, 47, 49, 50, 56, 63, 77, 78, 83–85, 87, 92, 93, 98, 101, 115, 134, 151, 161, 164, 173, 181, 183, 187
Cameron, James 19, 33
Carla Brody 31, 49, 58, 68, 69, 72, 74–76, 78, 81, 105–7, 109–14, 118, 119, 126, 127, 139–41, 143, 144, 187
Cinefantastique 28, 29, 55, 66, 89
Cocoon 37, 39, 190

D

DeJarnett, Steve 202
Dreyfuss, Richard 70, 87, 164, 183

E

Eastwood, Clint 88
Edgartown 15, 24, 26–28, 32, 33, 42, 44–46, 61, 67, 87, 172, 177, 187, 192–94
Ellen, Brody 19, 25, 30, 43, 44, 51, 52, 56, 59, 64, 67–83, 97, 99, 102–20,

122, 124–30, 134, 136, 138–45, 155, 159, 160, 172, 173

F

Fangoria 43, 51
Ferguson, Mrs 33, 76, 113, 153

G

Galactica, Battlestar 22
Gary, Lorraine 15, 19, 24, 25, 30, 36, 41, 43, 44, 49, 56, 59, 63, 64, 82, 83, 87, 93, 94, 98, 101, 103, 112, 137, 159, 162, 172, 184, 187
Ghostbusters 22, 34, 96, 166
Goonies, The 36, 123, 188
Guest, Lance 30–32, 34, 35, 40, 56, 57, 65, 71, 80, 81, 85, 92, 150, 173, 175, 187
Guzman, Michael De 20, 22, 25, 26, 52, 67, 71, 101, 108, 113, 115, 135, 161, 163, 176, 180, 189

H

Haley, Brendan 10, 202
Halloween 30, 34, 175
Hamman, Diana 63, 194, 202
Hancock, John D. 41, 135, 159, 160
Harlin, Renny 167
Hendricks, Deputy 34
Hetfield, Diane 33, 113
Hoagie 31, 53, 56, 61, 62, 64, 69–73, 75, 77–83, 106, 108–11, 114–20, 125, 126, 128, 129, 139–46, 183

J

Jake 31, 32, 62, 66, 69–72, 74, 75, 78–80, 82, 83, 87, 89, 91, 95, 98, 107–16, 118–22, 125, 126, 128–30, 140–42, 144, 145, 174
Jankiewicz, Pat 65
Jarnatt 22, 23
Jaws 9–13, 15, 16, 19–52, 56, 57, 59, 60, 62, 65, 67, 71, 74, 76, 78, 80, 83–103, 108, 110, 113–18, 121, 123–25, 127, 129, 130, 132, 133, 135–38, 146, 147, 150, 153–67, 172, 175, 176, 182–84, 186–88, 190–94, 196
Jeannot, Szwarc 41, 160

L

Lawrence, Tim 28, 66, 90

M

Mankiewicz, Tom 62
McPherson, John 35, 45, 53–55, 61, 64, 181
Millar, Henry and Mike 27, 28, 39, 48, 101

N

Newcombe, Hoagie 31
Nishizawa, Ryuichi 156, 157, 202
novelisation 12, 16, 68, 71, 77, 111, 135–38, 146, 183

P

Peebles, Mario Van 30, 31, 50, 56, 57, 59, 65, 74, 79, 80, 87–89, 98, 113

Q

Quint 16, 25, 82, 155

R

Rae, Ted 28, 39, 55, 66, 90, 194–96

S

Sakamoto, Shinichi 154, 157
Sargent, Joseph 11, 19, 20, 22, 25, 26, 28, 29, 35, 37, 39, 43, 46, 51–53, 55, 59, 61, 62, 64, 66, 79, 82, 86, 89, 90, 92, 101–4, 107, 109, 111–13, 115, 116, 132–34, 136, 162, 172, 176, 184, 185, 189, 191, 196
Scheider, Roy 11, 25, 26, 30, 36, 40, 41, 51, 70, 87, 92, 123, 133, 164
Sheinberg, Sid and Lorraine 15, 19, 20, 22–24, 26, 43, 49, 65, 132, 133, 159–63, 177, 182, 190
Spielberg, Steven 11, 16, 19, 20, 24–26, 33, 35, 86, 87, 94, 156, 157, 159, 162, 172
Statham, Jason 170

U

universal 11, 15, 17, 20, 22–27, 30, 35, 41, 42, 44, 50, 51, 55, 60–66, 70, 84, 85, 88, 89, 116, 118, 121, 155, 159, 160, 162, 163, 174, 175, 178, 180, 181, 184, 186, 188, 190, 195

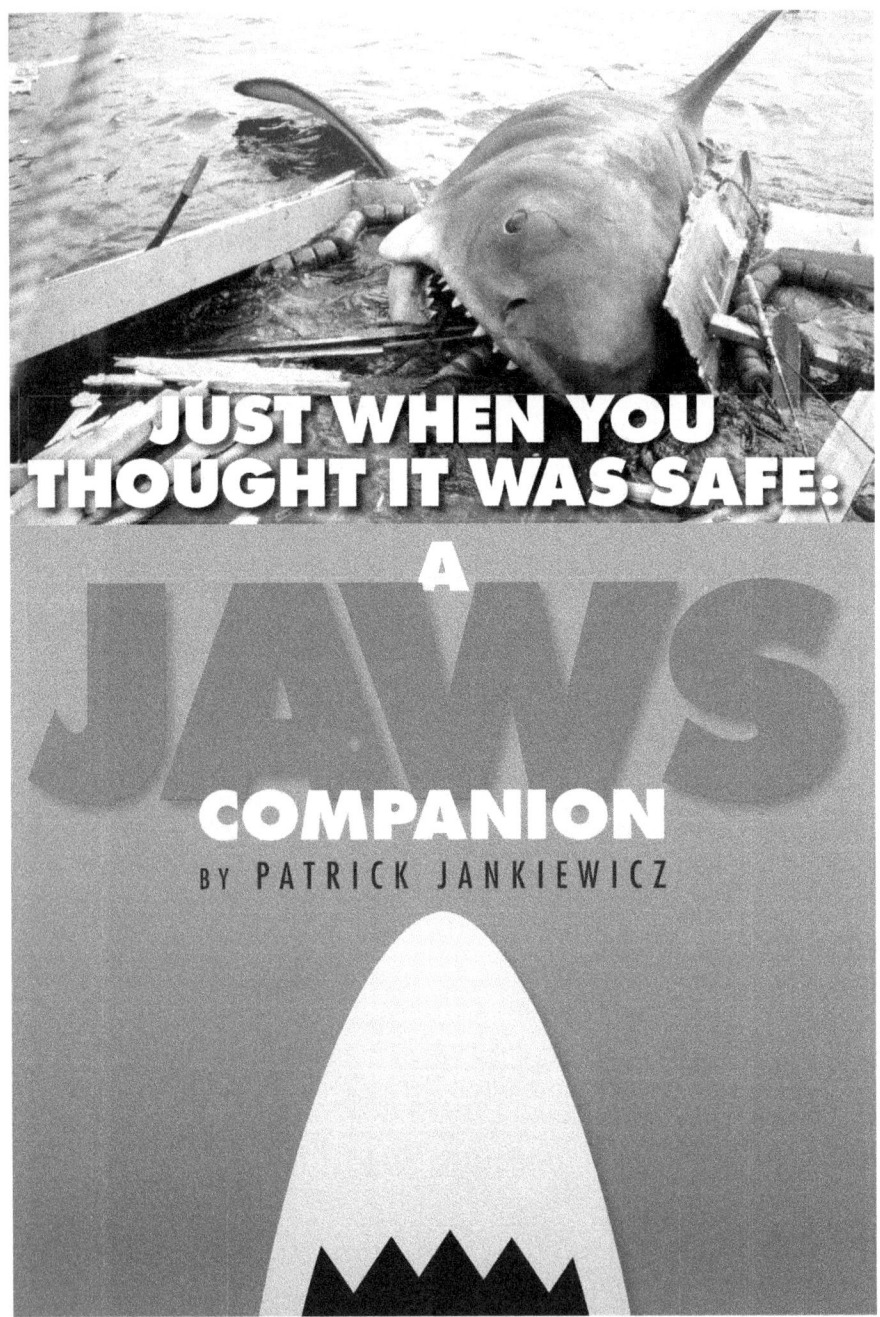

www.ingramcontent.com/pod-product-compliance
Lightning Source LLC
Chambersburg PA
CBHW071444150426
43191CB00008B/1237